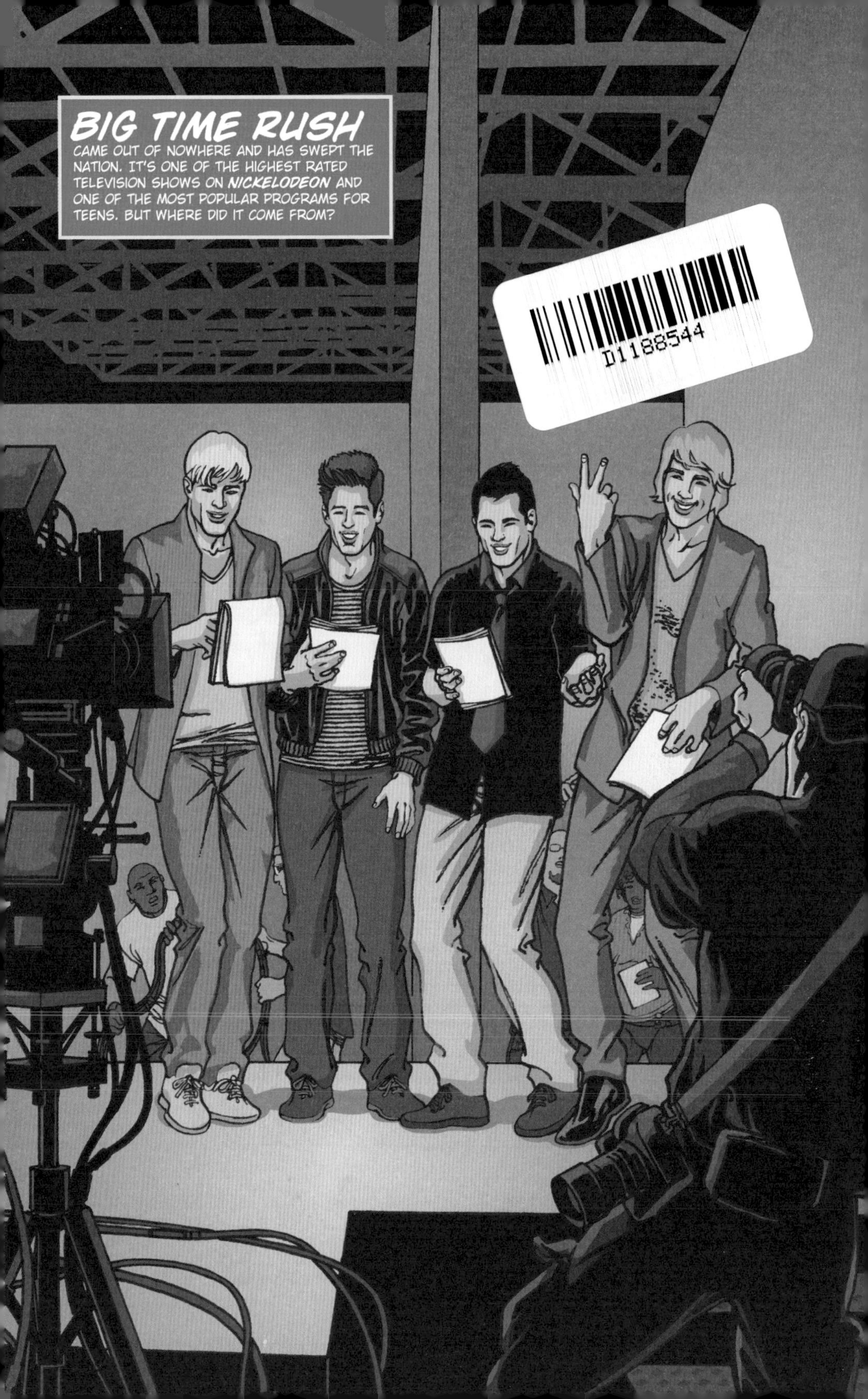
BIG TIME RUSH
CAME OUT OF NOWHERE AND HAS SWEPT THE NATION. IT'S ONE OF THE HIGHEST RATED TELEVISION SHOWS ON NICKELODEON AND ONE OF THE MOST POPULAR PROGRAMS FOR TEENS. BUT WHERE DID IT COME FROM?

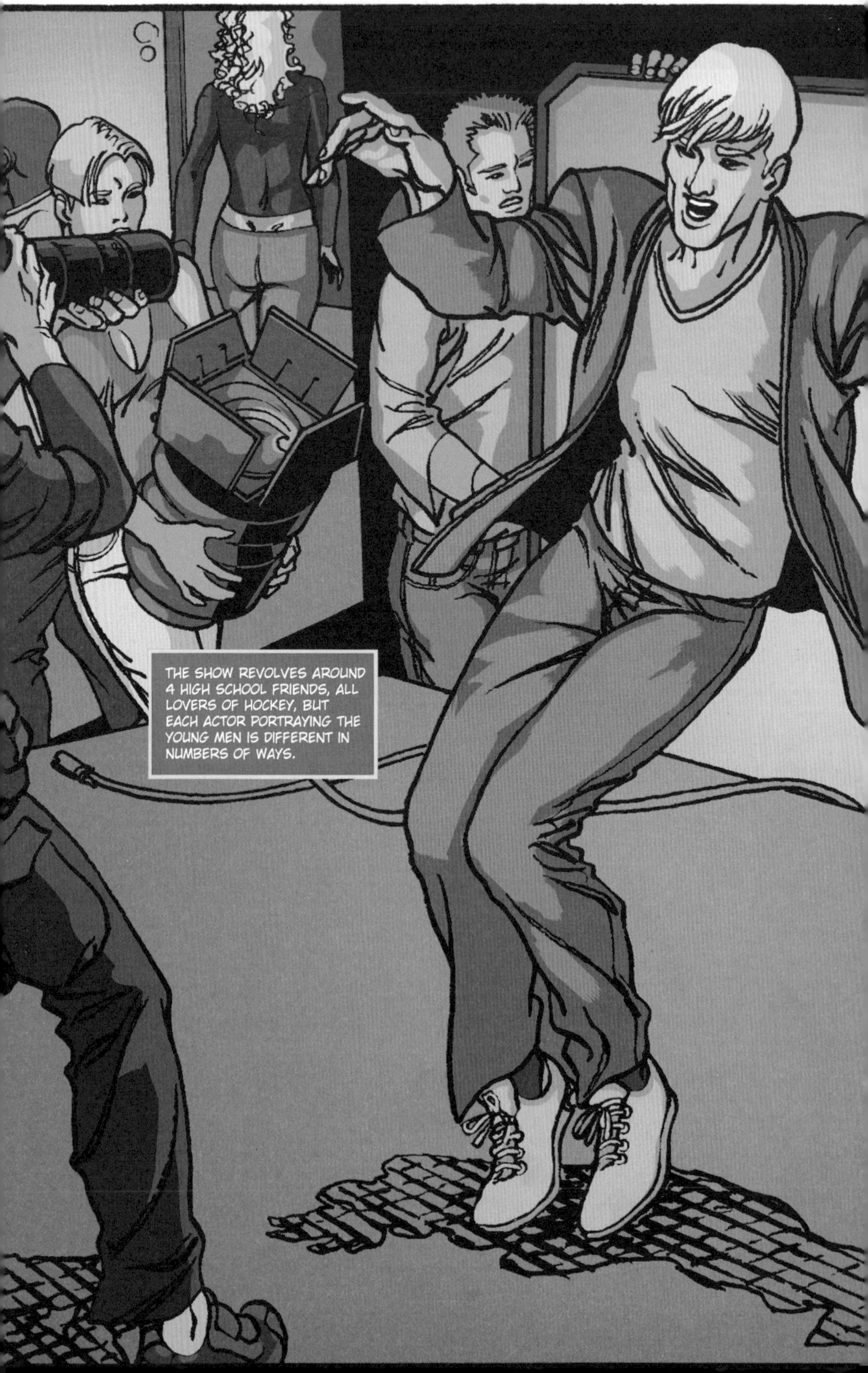
THE SHOW REVOLVES AROUND 4 HIGH SCHOOL FRIENDS, ALL LOVERS OF HOCKEY, BUT EACH ACTOR PORTRAYING THE YOUNG MEN IS DIFFERENT IN NUMBERS OF WAYS.

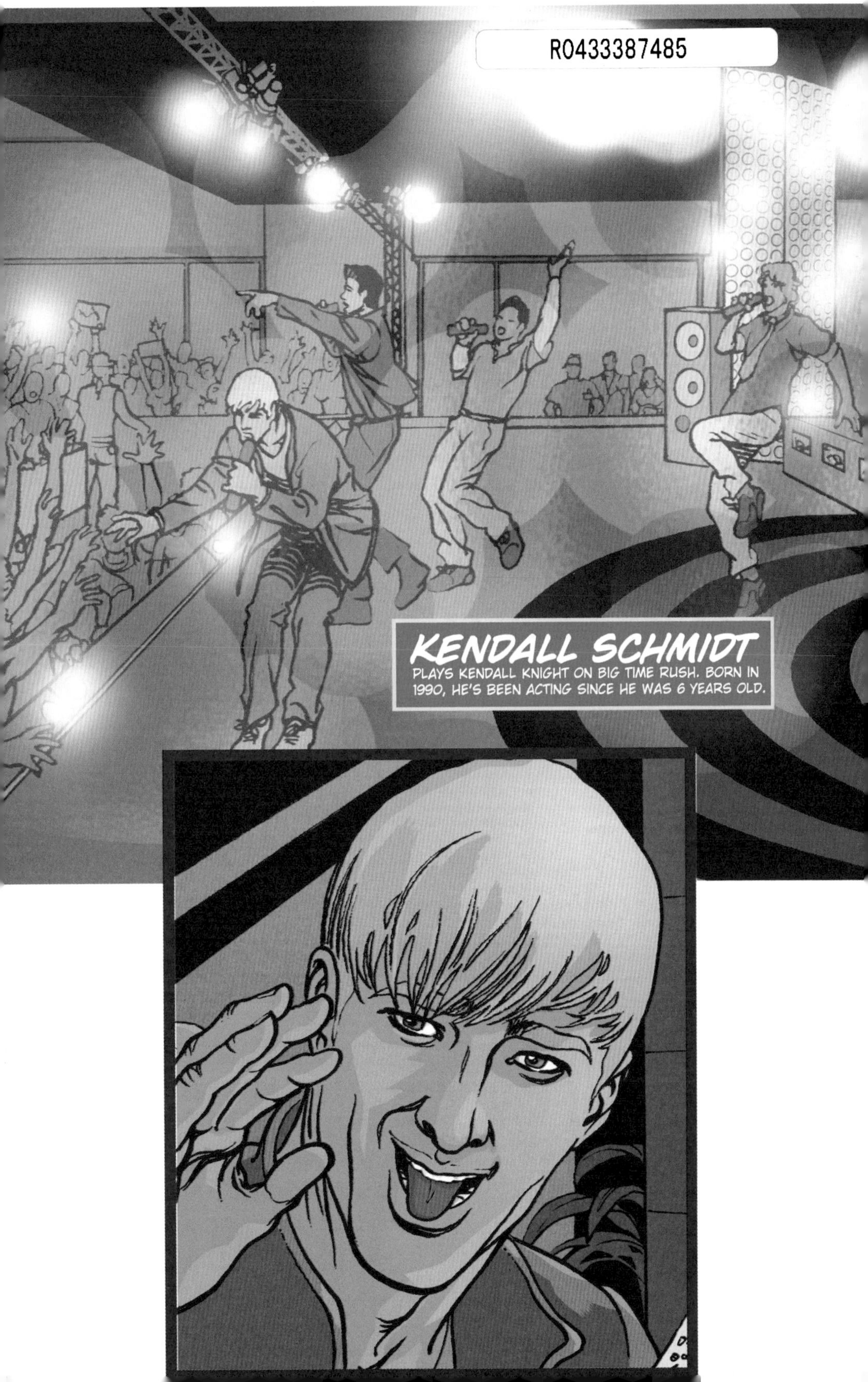
KENDALL SCHMIDT
PLAYS KENDALL KNIGHT ON BIG TIME RUSH. BORN IN 1990, HE'S BEEN ACTING SINCE HE WAS 6 YEARS OLD.

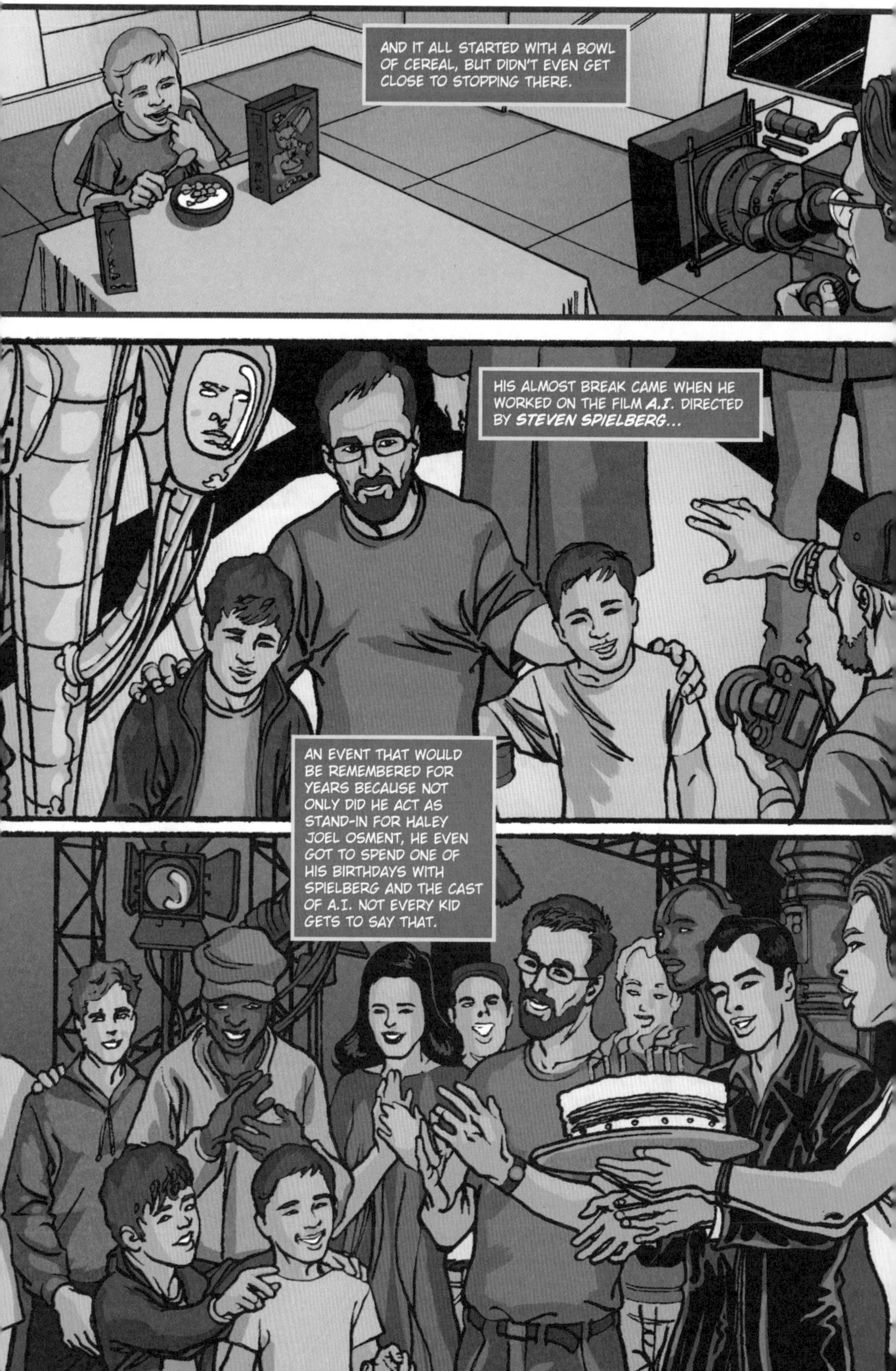
AND IT ALL STARTED WITH A BOWL OF CEREAL, BUT DIDN'T EVEN GET CLOSE TO STOPPING THERE.
HIS ALMOST BREAK CAME WHEN HE WORKED ON THE FILM ***A.I.*** DIRECTED BY ***STEVEN SPIELBERG...***
AN EVENT THAT WOULD BE REMEMBERED FOR YEARS BECAUSE NOT ONLY DID HE ACT AS STAND-IN FOR HALEY JOEL OSMENT, HE EVEN GOT TO SPEND ONE OF HIS BIRTHDAYS WITH SPIELBERG AND THE CAST OF A.I. NOT EVERY KID GETS TO SAY THAT.

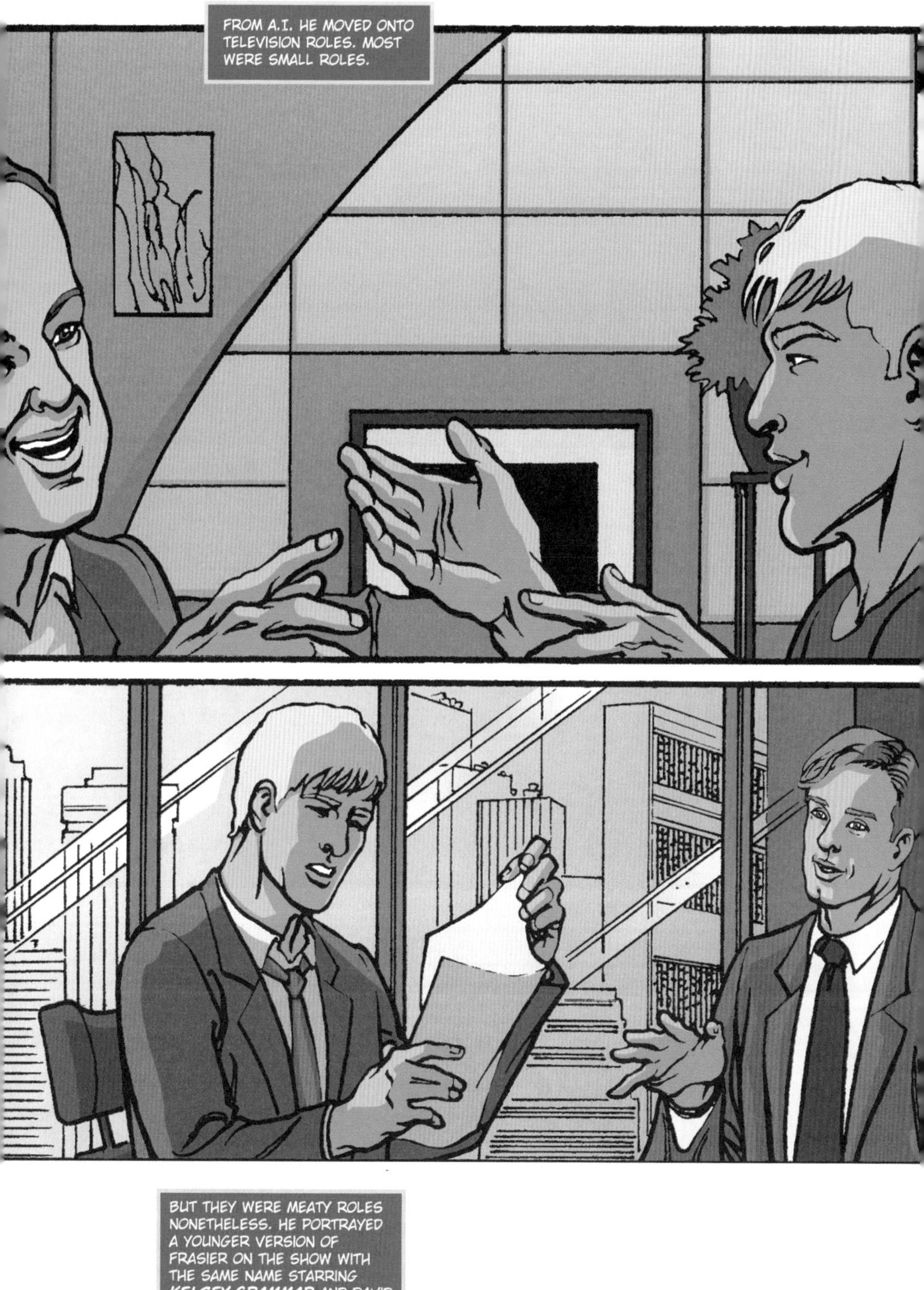
FROM A.I. HE MOVED ONTO TELEVISION ROLES. MOST WERE SMALL ROLES.
BUT THEY WERE MEATY ROLES NONETHELESS. HE PORTRAYED A YOUNGER VERSION OF FRASIER ON THE SHOW WITH THE SAME NAME STARRING
KELSEY GRAMMAR AND DAVID HYDE PIERCE.

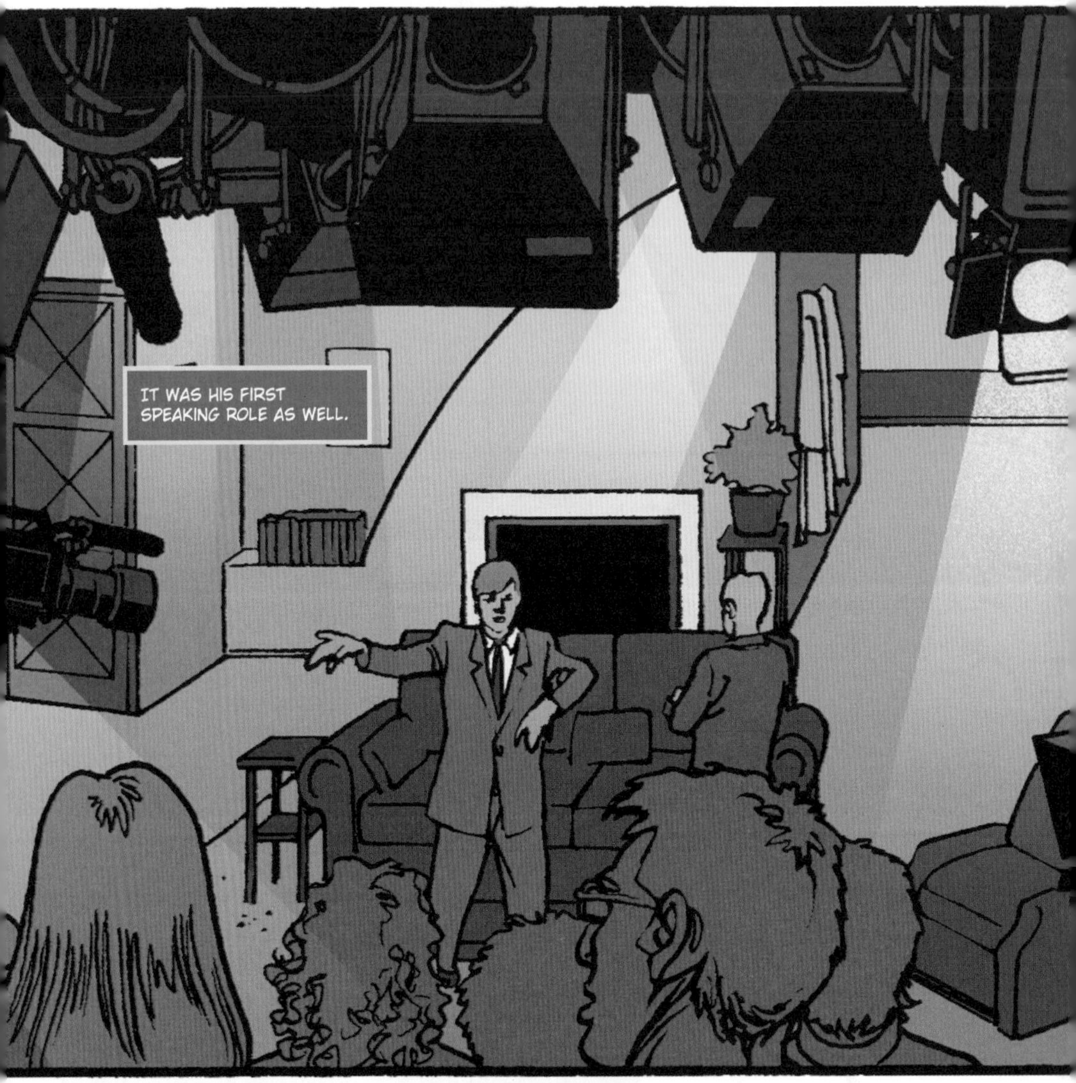
IT WAS HIS FIRST SPEAKING ROLE AS WELL.

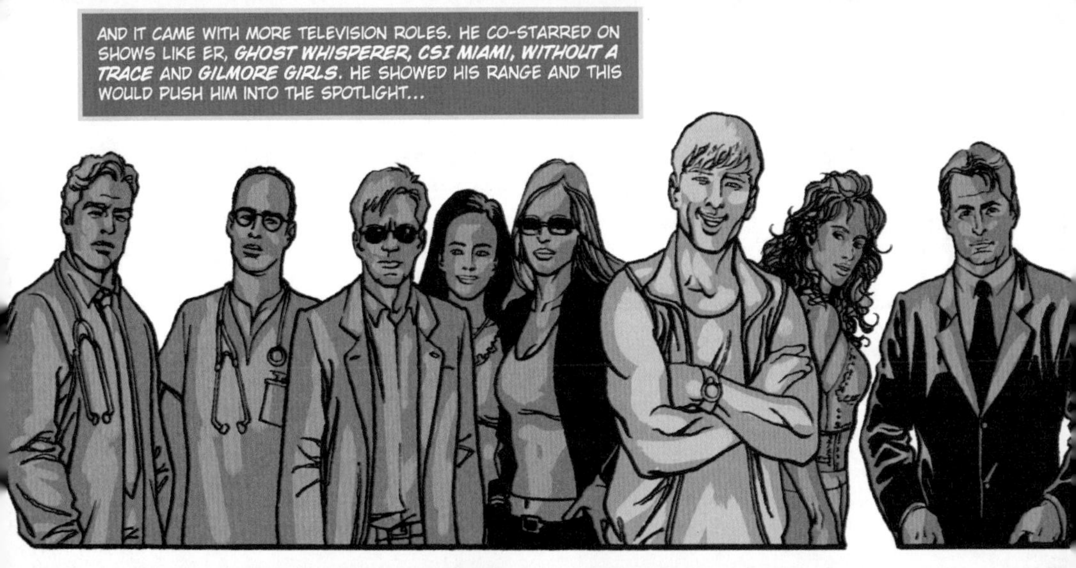
AND IT CAME WITH MORE TELEVISION ROLES. HE CO-STARRED ON SHOWS LIKE ER, GHOST WHISPERER, CSI MIAMI, WITHOUT A TRACE AND GILMORE GIRLS. HE SHOWED HIS RANGE AND THIS WOULD PUSH HIM INTO THE SPOTLIGHT...

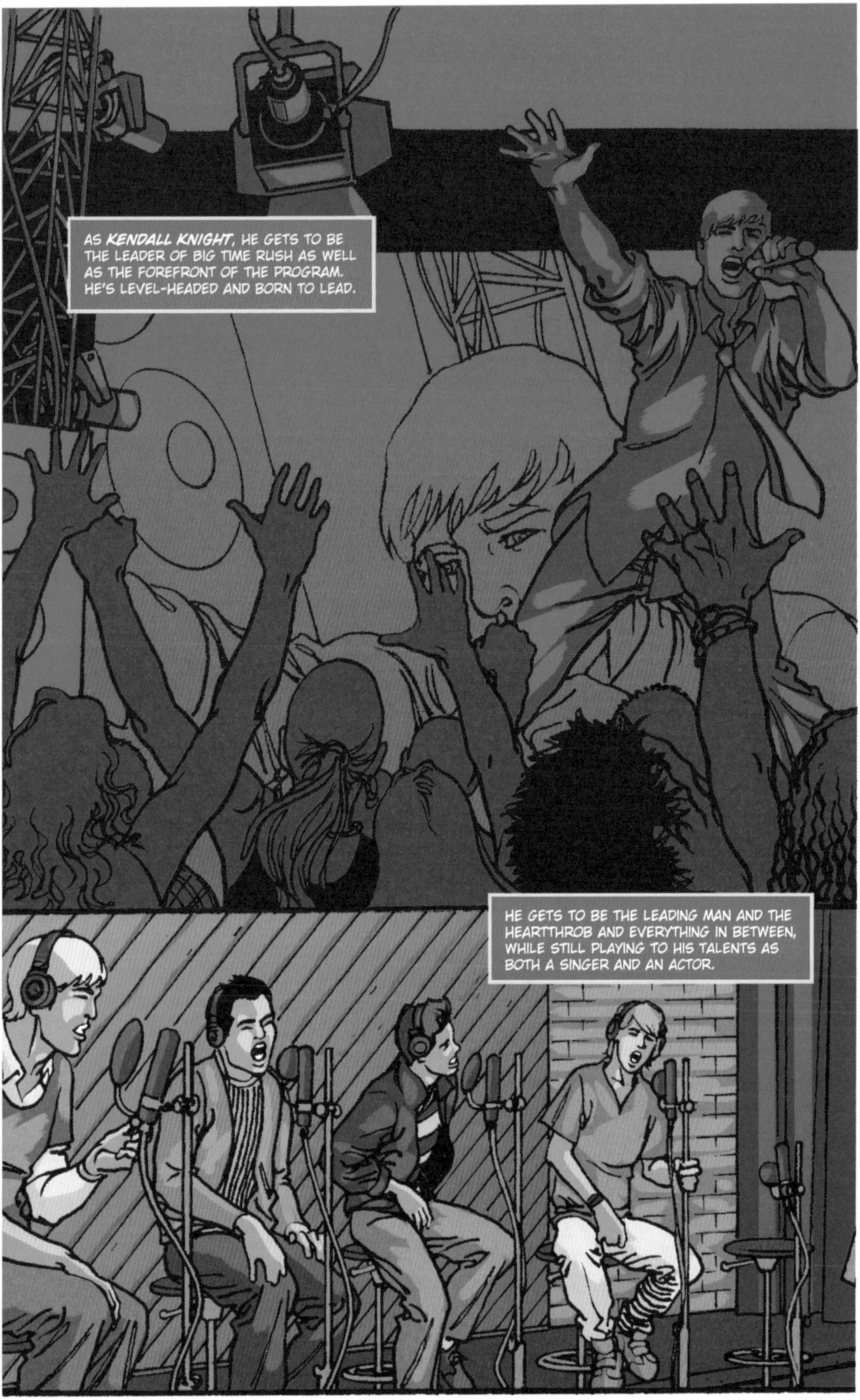
AS KENDALL KNIGHT, HE GETS TO BE THE LEADER OF BIG TIME RUSH AS WELL AS THE FOREFRONT OF THE PROGRAM. HE'S LEVEL-HEADED AND BORN TO LEAD.
HE GETS TO BE THE LEADING MAN AND THE HEARTTHROB AND EVERYTHING IN BETWEEN, WHILE STILL PLAYING TO HIS TALENTS AS BOTH A SINGER AND AN ACTOR.

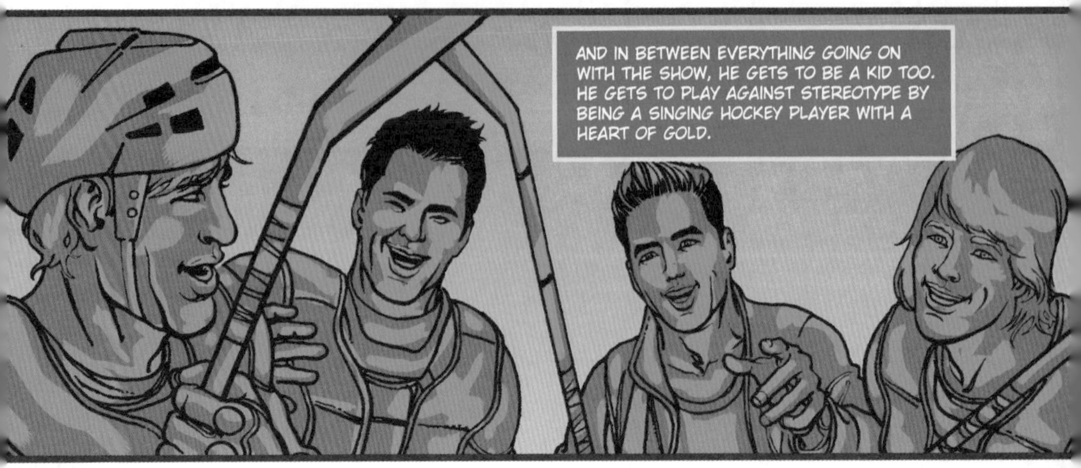
AND IN BETWEEN EVERYTHING GOING ON WITH THE SHOW, HE GETS TO BE A KID TOO. HE GETS TO PLAY AGAINST STEREOTYPE BY BEING A SINGING HOCKEY PLAYER WITH A HEART OF GOLD.

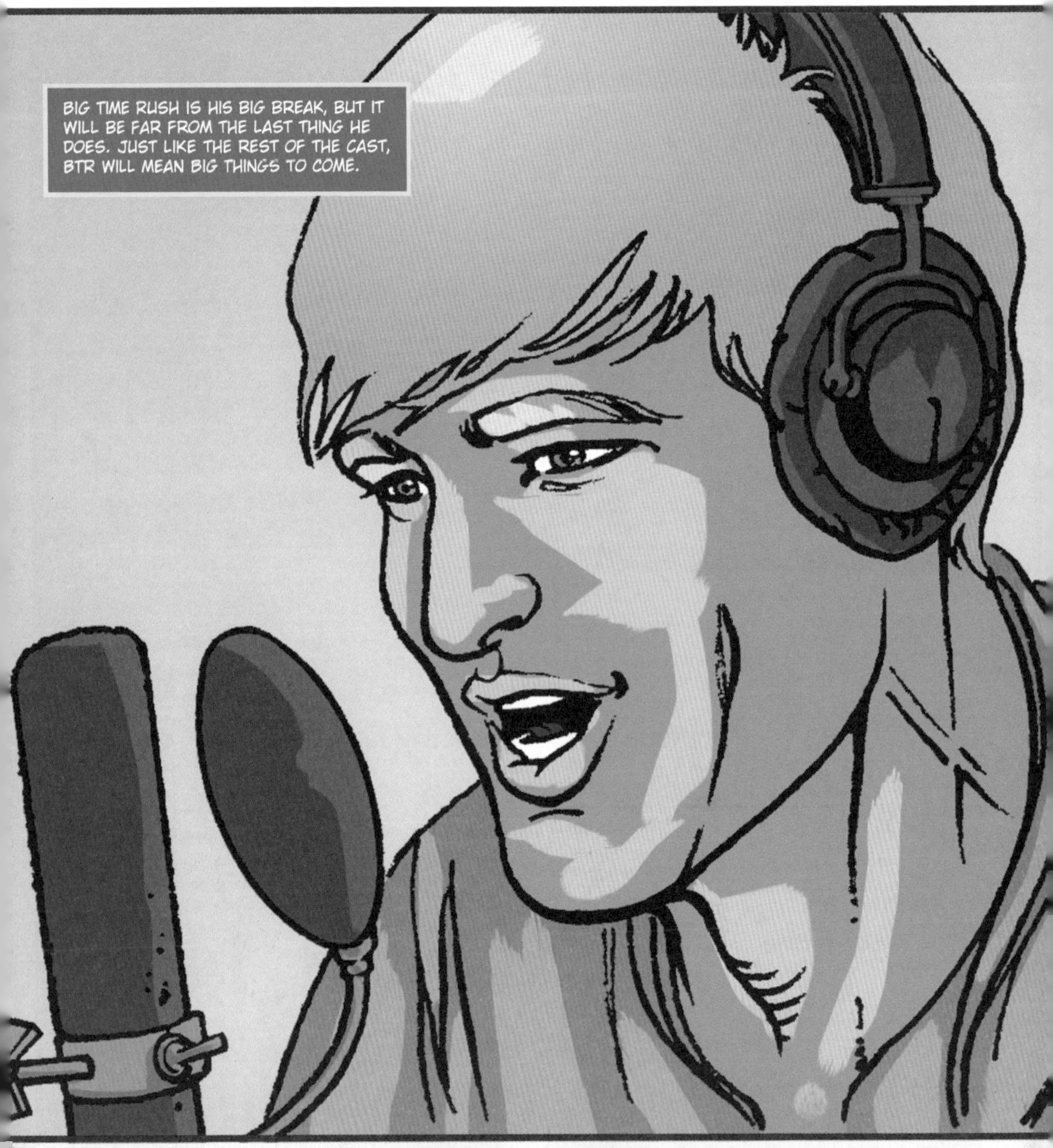
BIG TIME RUSH IS HIS BIG BREAK, BUT IT WILL BE FAR FROM THE LAST THING HE DOES. JUST LIKE THE REST OF THE CAST, BTR WILL MEAN BIG THINGS TO COME.

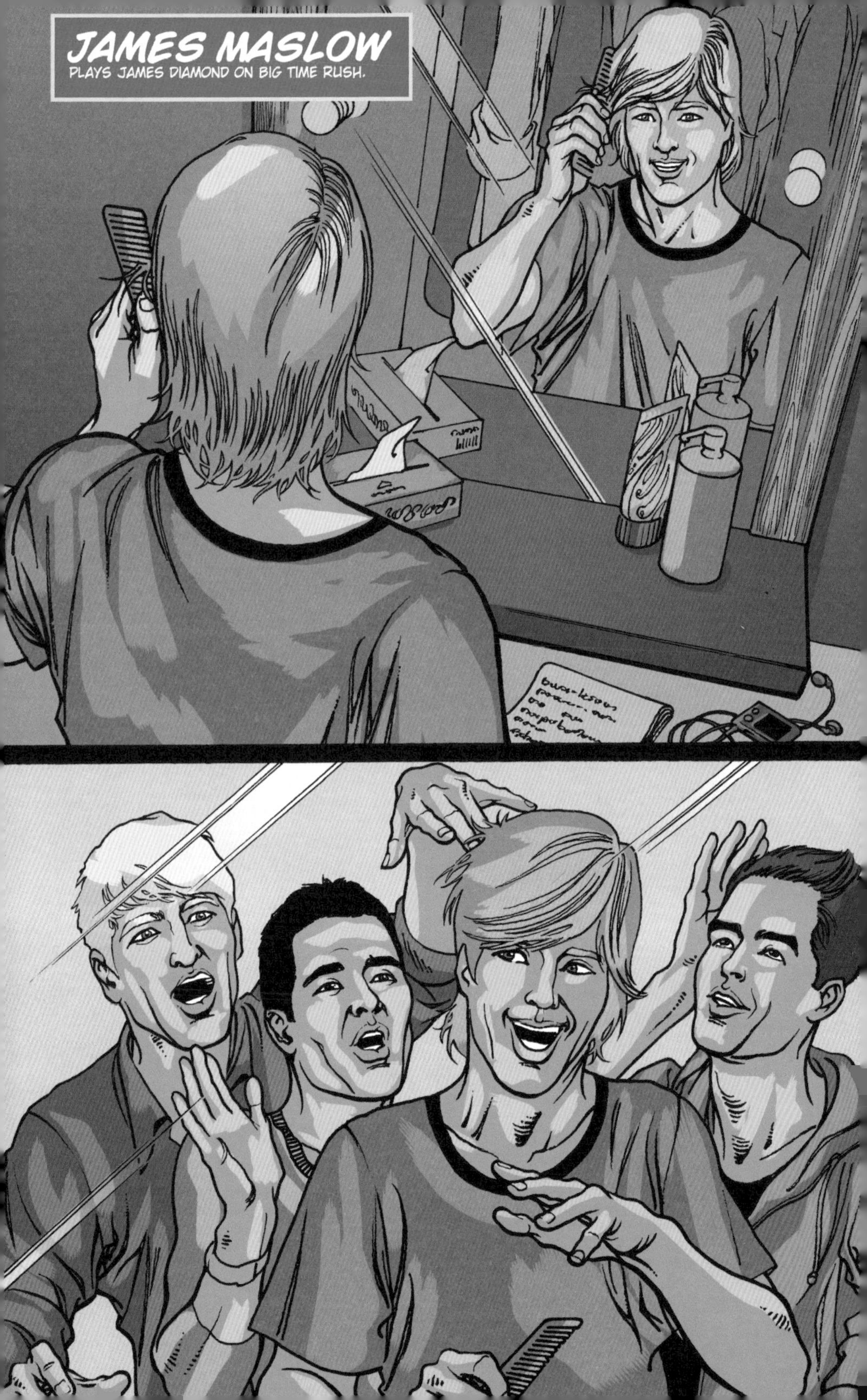
JAMES MASLOW
PLAYS JAMES DIAMOND ON BIG TIME RUSH.

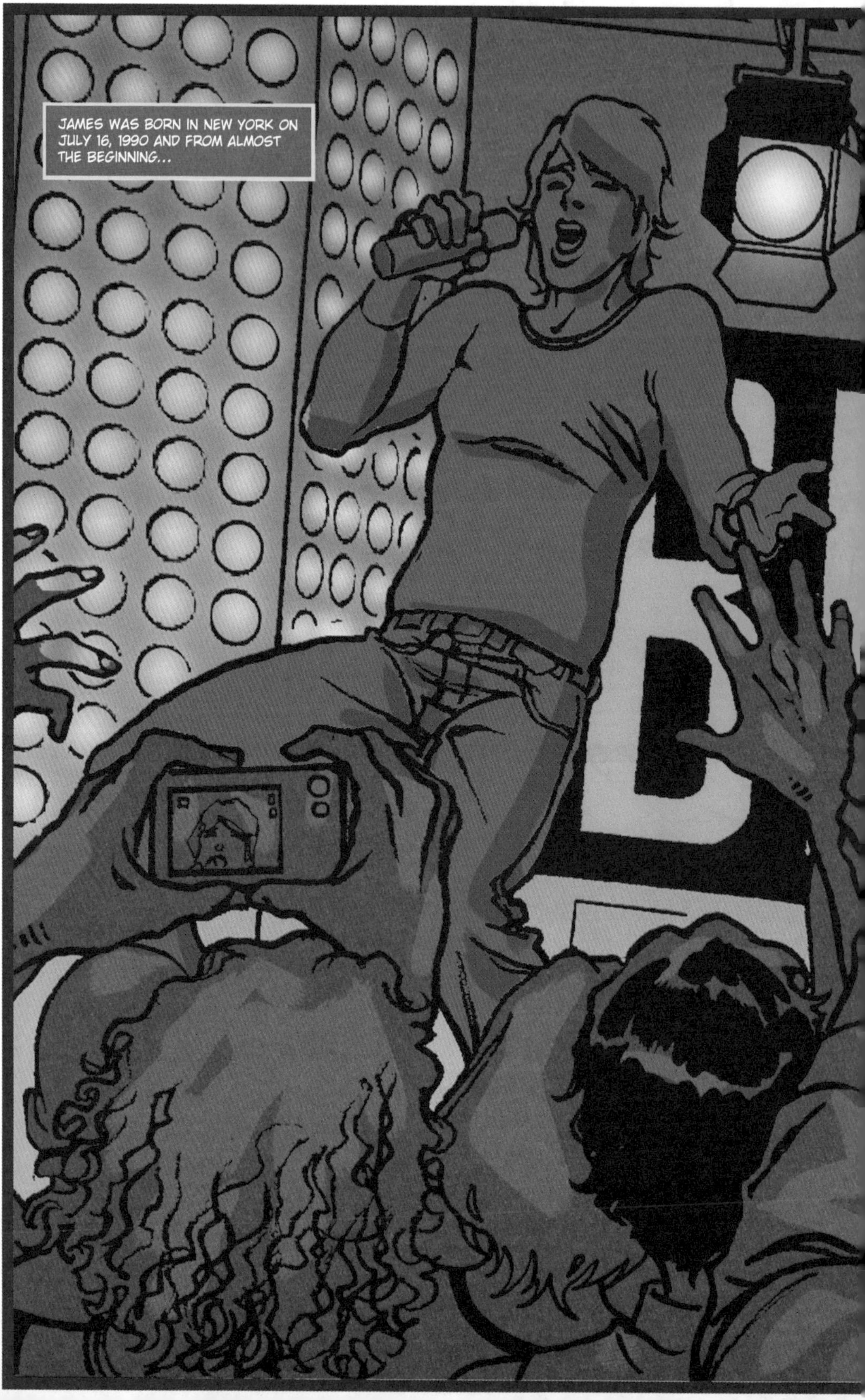
JAMES WAS BORN IN NEW YORK ON JULY 16, 1990 AND FROM ALMOST THE BEGINNING...

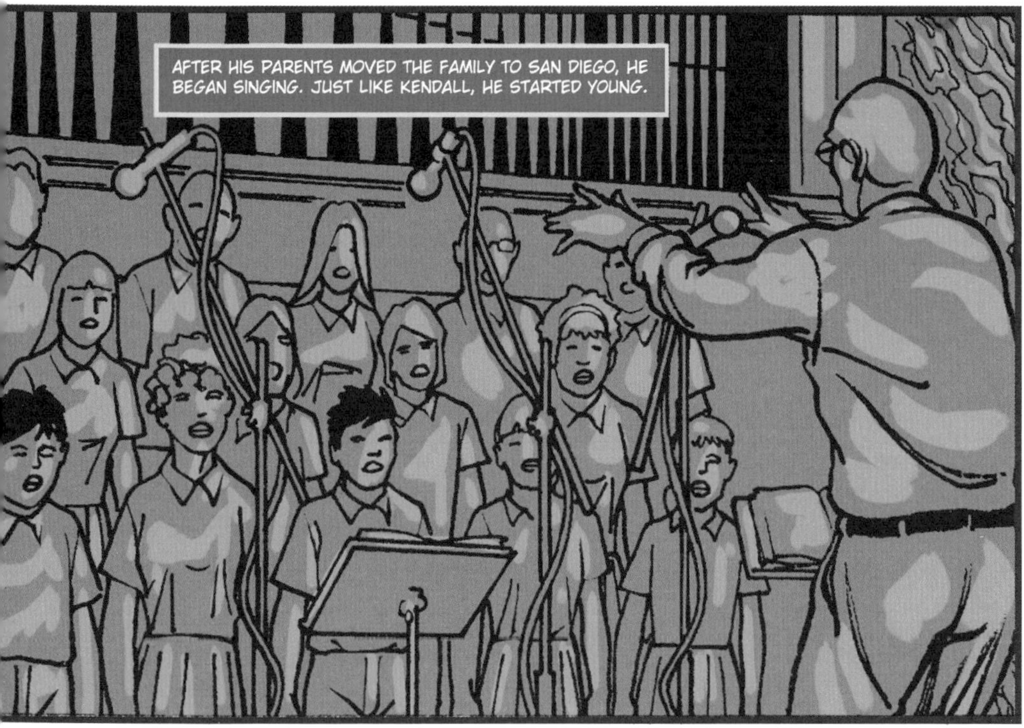
AFTER HIS PARENTS MOVED THE FAMILY TO SAN DIEGO, HE BEGAN SINGING. JUST LIKE KENDALL, HE STARTED YOUNG.

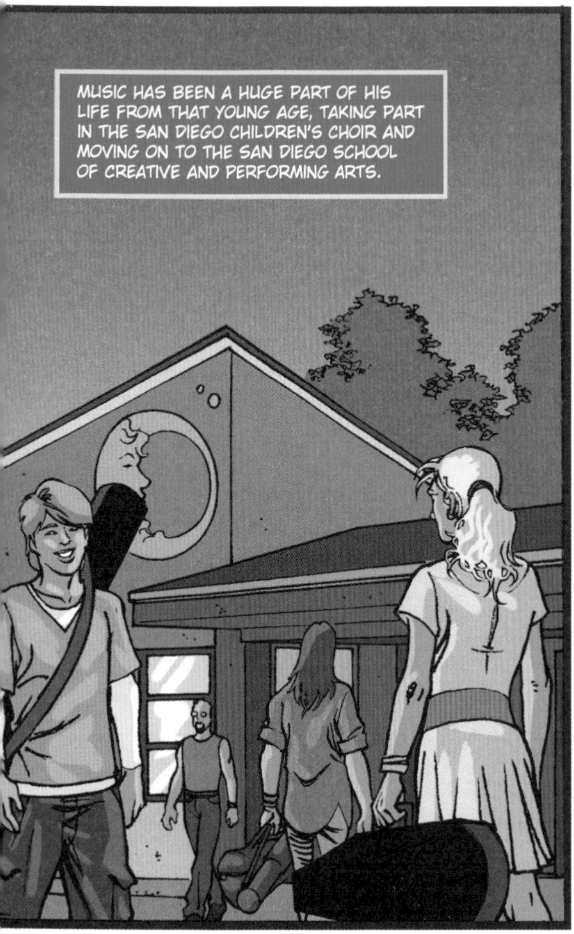
MUSIC HAS BEEN A HUGE PART OF HIS LIFE FROM THAT YOUNG AGE, TAKING PART IN THE SAN DIEGO CHILDREN'S CHOIR AND MOVING ON TO THE SAN DIEGO SCHOOL OF CREATIVE AND PERFORMING ARTS.

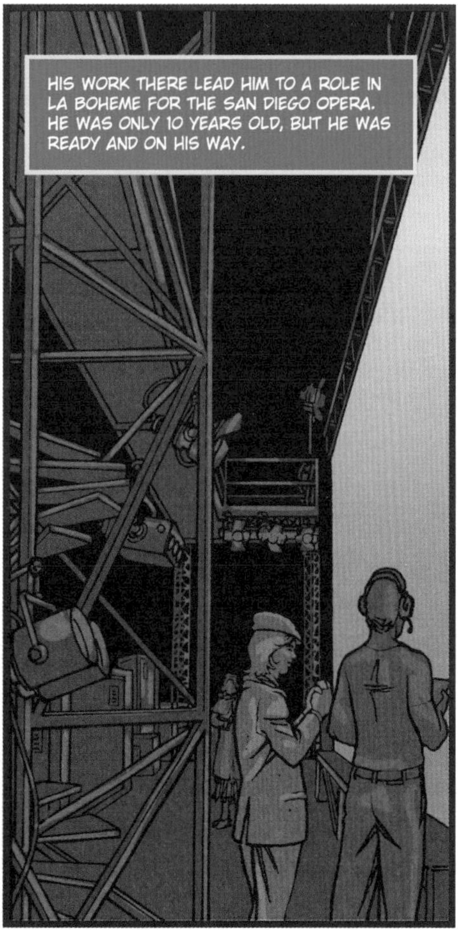
HIS WORK THERE LEAD HIM TO A ROLE IN LA BOHEME FOR THE SAN DIEGO OPERA. HE WAS ONLY 10 YEARS OLD, BUT HE WAS READY AND ON HIS WAY.

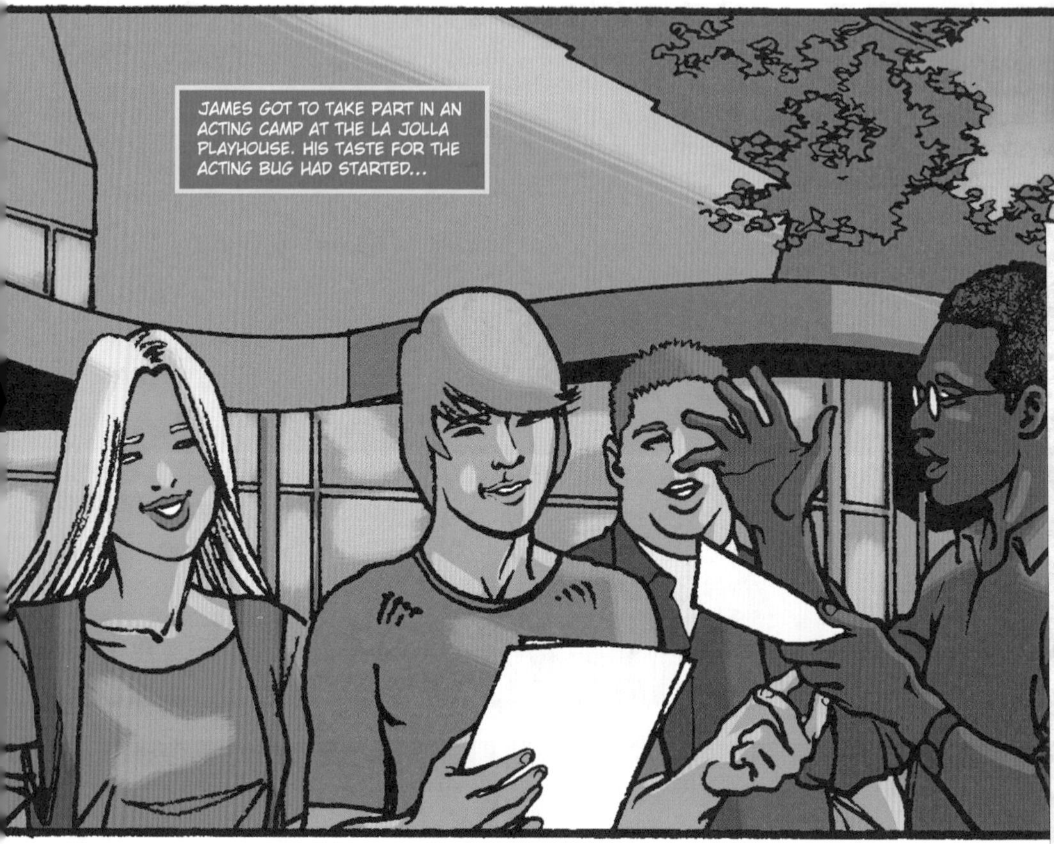
JAMES GOT TO TAKE PART IN AN ACTING CAMP AT THE LA JOLLA PLAYHOUSE. HIS TASTE FOR THE ACTING BUG HAD STARTED...

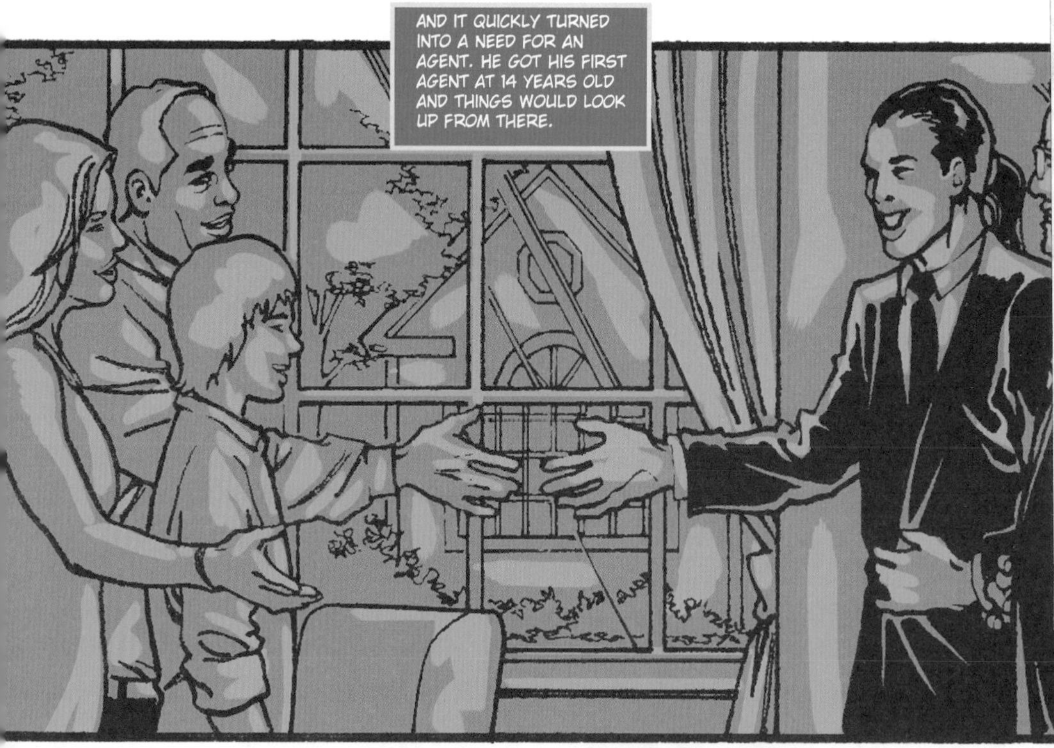
AND IT QUICKLY TURNED INTO A NEED FOR AN AGENT. HE GOT HIS FIRST AGENT AT 14 YEARS OLD AND THINGS WOULD LOOK UP FROM THERE.

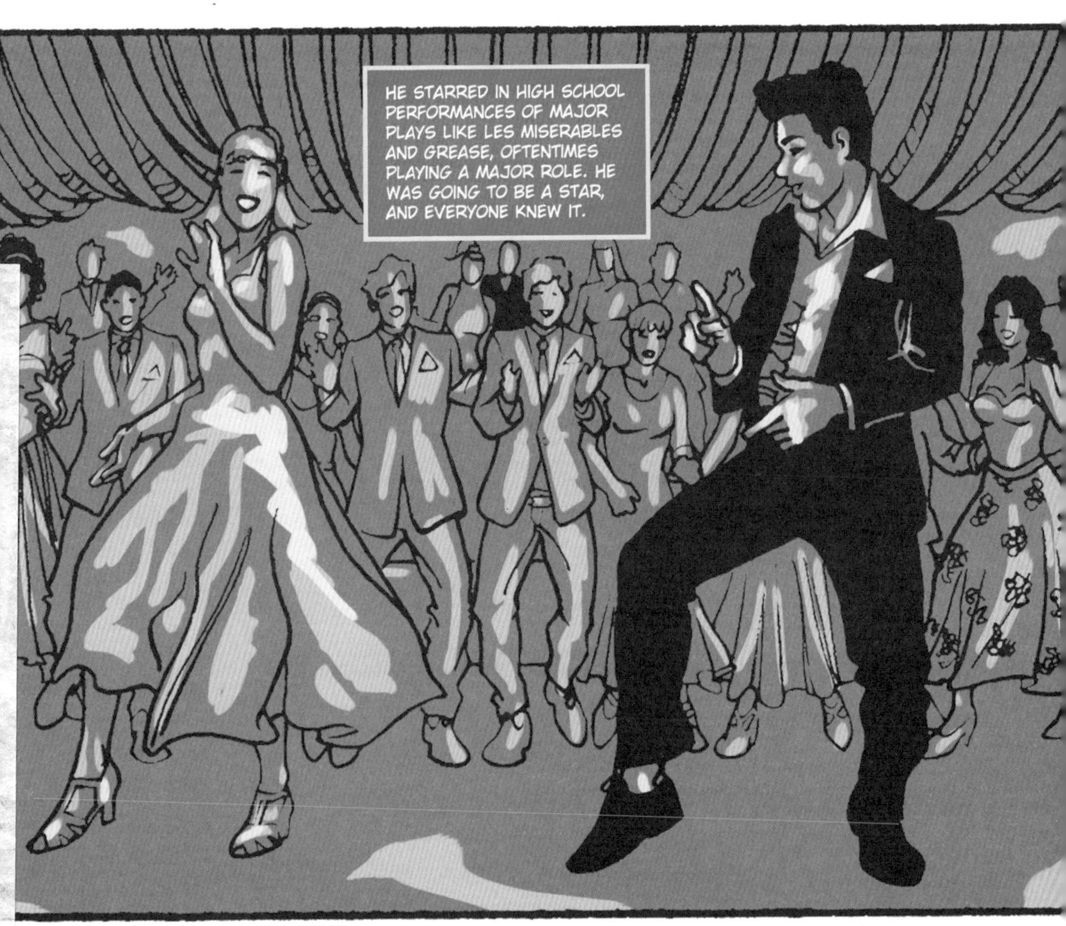
HE STARRED IN HIGH SCHOOL PERFORMANCES OF MAJOR PLAYS LIKE LES MISERABLES AND GREASE, OFTENTIMES PLAYING A MAJOR ROLE. HE WAS GOING TO BE A STAR, AND EVERYONE KNEW IT.

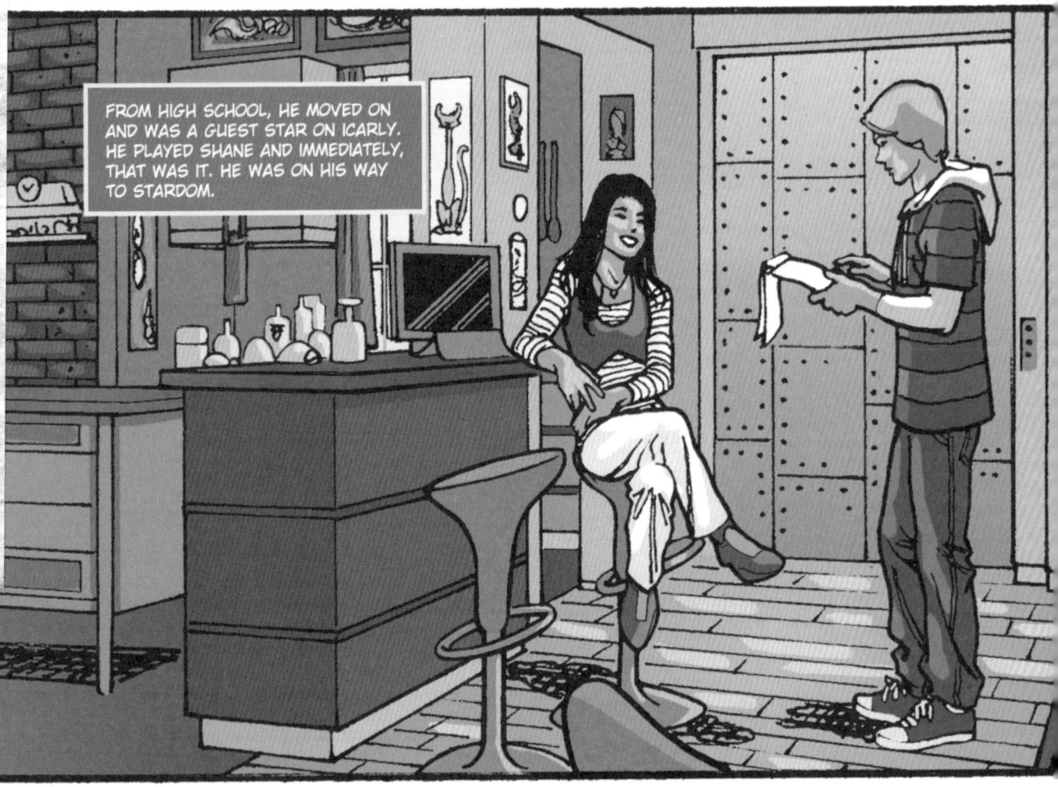
FROM HIGH SCHOOL, HE MOVED ON AND WAS A GUEST STAR ON ICARLY. HE PLAYED SHANE AND IMMEDIATELY, THAT WAS IT. HE WAS ON HIS WAY TO STARDOM.

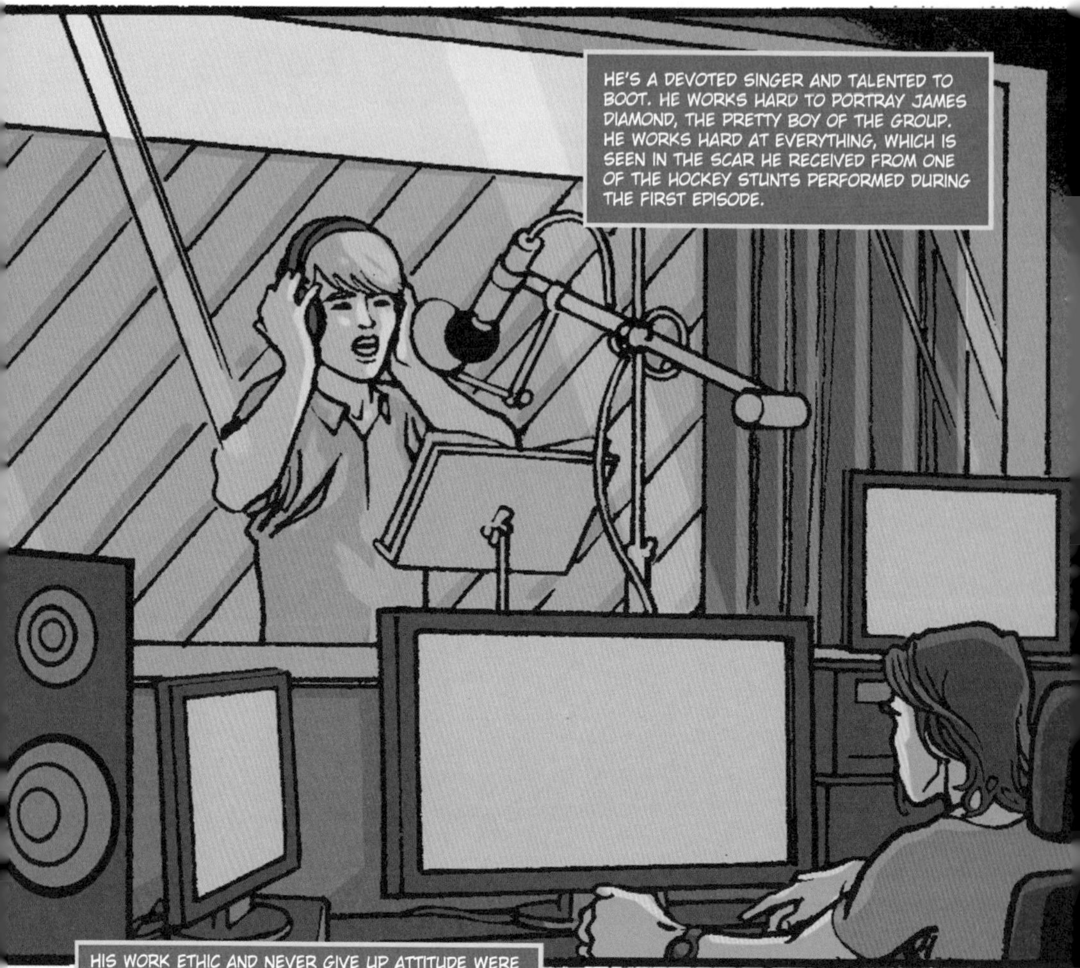
HE'S A DEVOTED SINGER AND TALENTED TO BOOT. HE WORKS HARD TO PORTRAY JAMES DIAMOND, THE PRETTY BOY OF THE GROUP. HE WORKS HARD AT EVERYTHING, WHICH IS SEEN IN THE SCAR HE RECEIVED FROM ONE OF THE HOCKEY STUNTS PERFORMED DURING THE FIRST EPISODE.

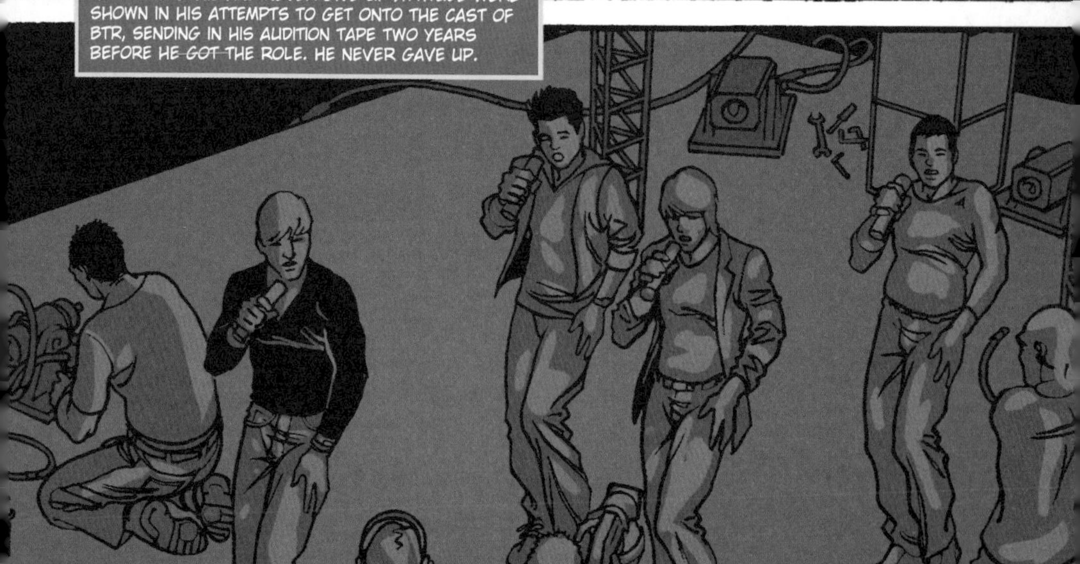
HIS WORK ETHIC AND NEVER GIVE UP ATTITUDE WERE SHOWN IN HIS ATTEMPTS TO GET ONTO THE CAST OF BTR, SENDING IN HIS AUDITION TAPE TWO YEARS BEFORE HE GOT THE ROLE. HE NEVER GAVE UP.

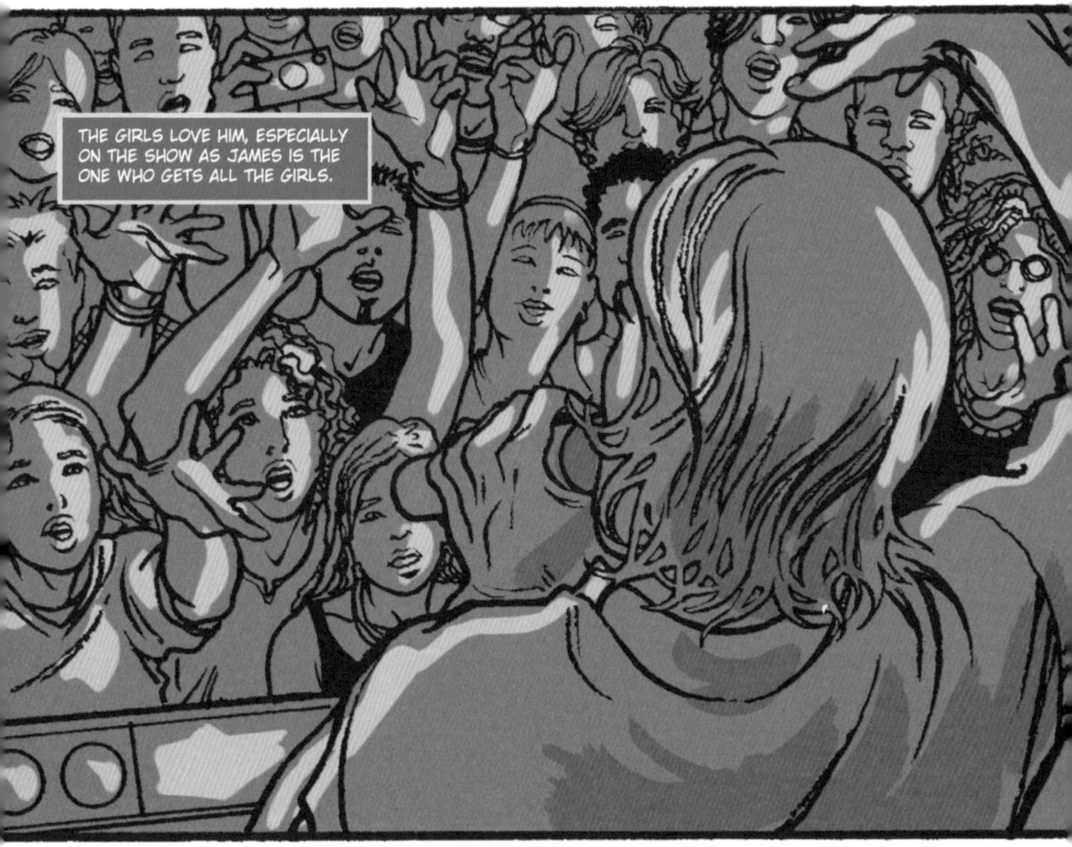
THE GIRLS LOVE HIM, ESPECIALLY ON THE SHOW AS JAMES IS THE ONE WHO GETS ALL THE GIRLS.

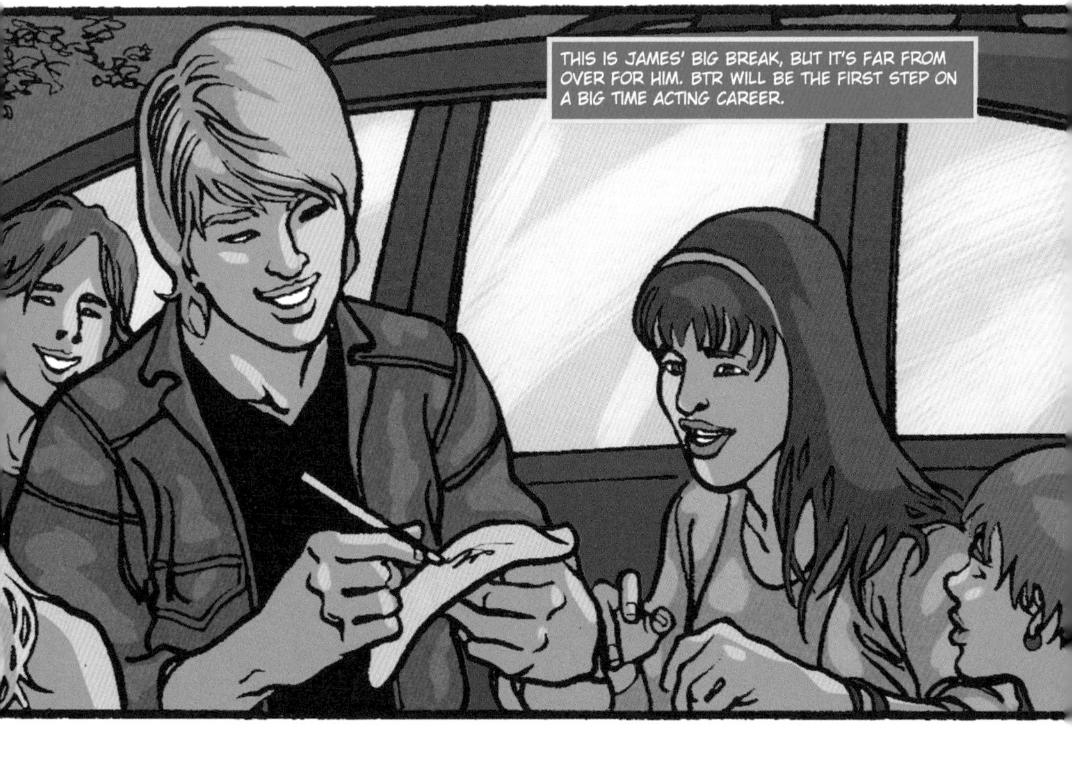
THIS IS JAMES' BIG BREAK, BUT IT'S FAR FROM OVER FOR HIM. BTR WILL BE THE FIRST STEP ON A BIG TIME ACTING CAREER.

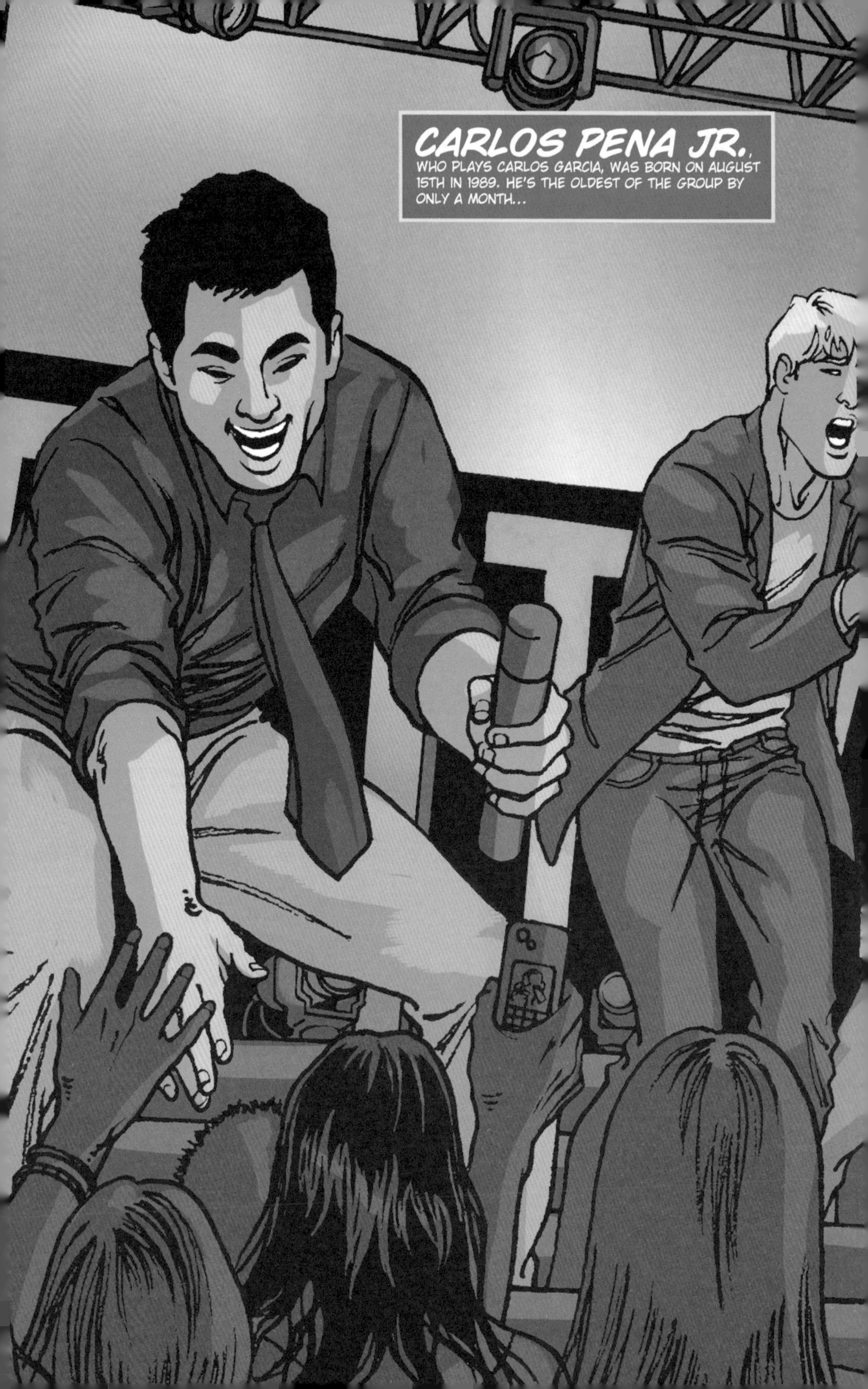
CARLOS PENA JR.,
WHO PLAYS CARLOS GARCIA, WAS BORN ON AUGUST 15TH IN 1989. HE'S THE OLDEST OF THE GROUP BY ONLY A MONTH...

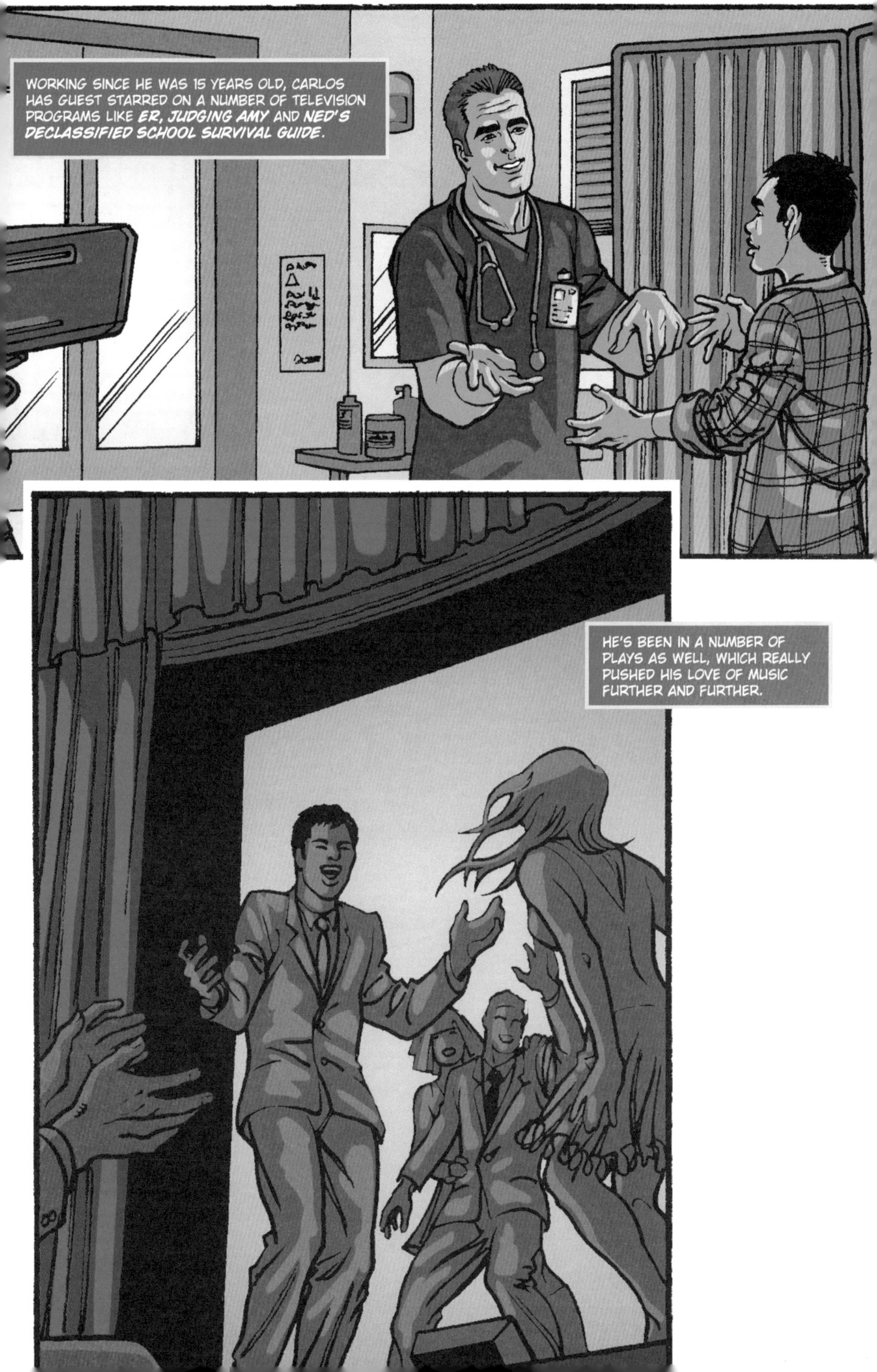
WORKING SINCE HE WAS 15 YEARS OLD, CARLOS HAS GUEST STARRED ON A NUMBER OF TELEVISION PROGRAMS LIKE ***ER, JUDGING AMY*** AND ***NED'S DECLASSIFIED SCHOOL SURVIVAL GUIDE***.
HE'S BEEN IN A NUMBER OF PLAYS AS WELL, WHICH REALLY PUSHED HIS LOVE OF MUSIC FURTHER AND FURTHER.

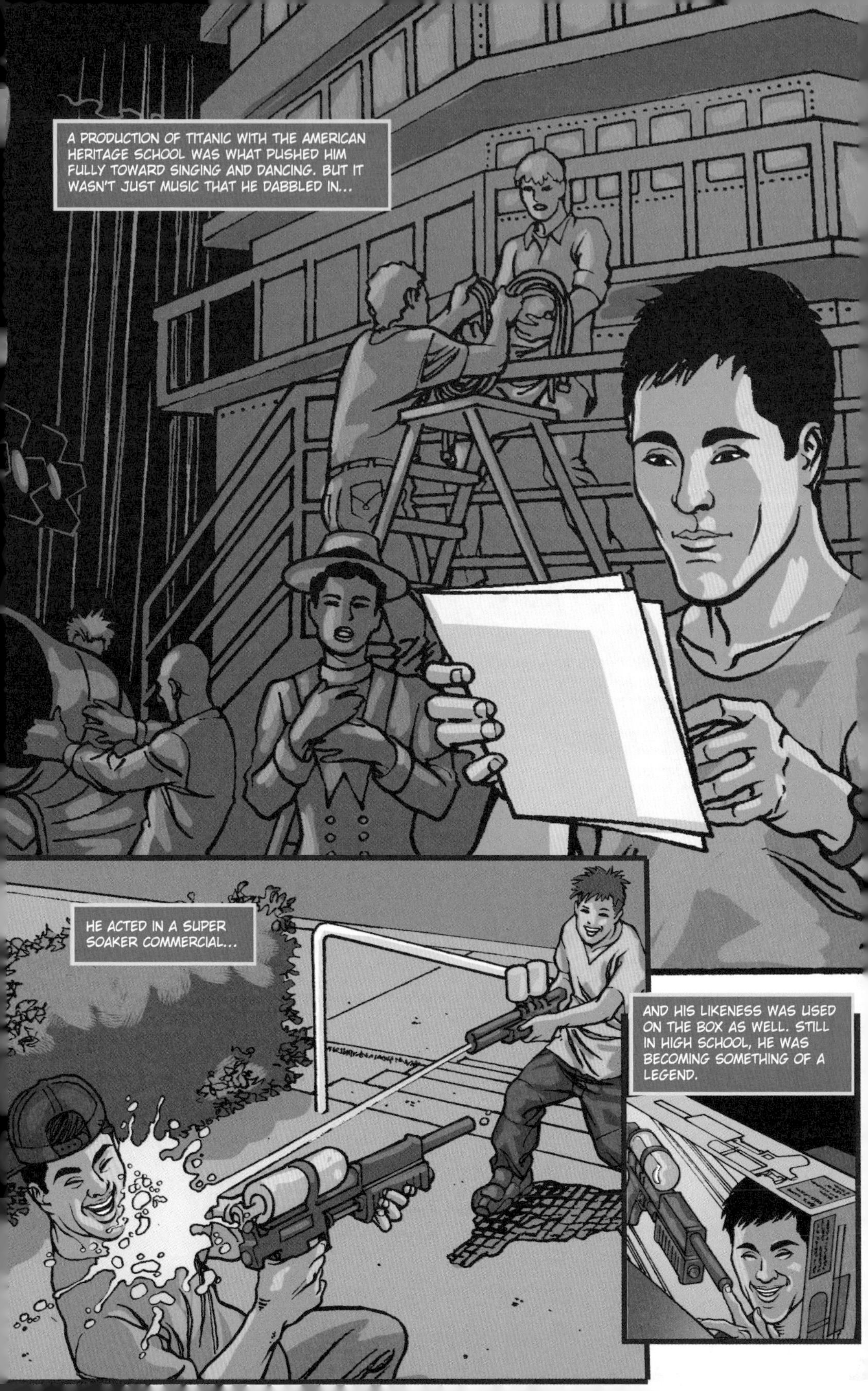
A PRODUCTION OF TITANIC WITH THE AMERICAN HERITAGE SCHOOL WAS WHAT PUSHED HIM FULLY TOWARD SINGING AND DANCING. BUT IT WASN'T JUST MUSIC THAT HE DABBLED IN...
HE ACTED IN A SUPER SOAKER COMMERCIAL...
AND HIS LIKENESS WAS USED ON THE BOX AS WELL. STILL IN HIGH SCHOOL, HE WAS BECOMING SOMETHING OF A LEGEND.

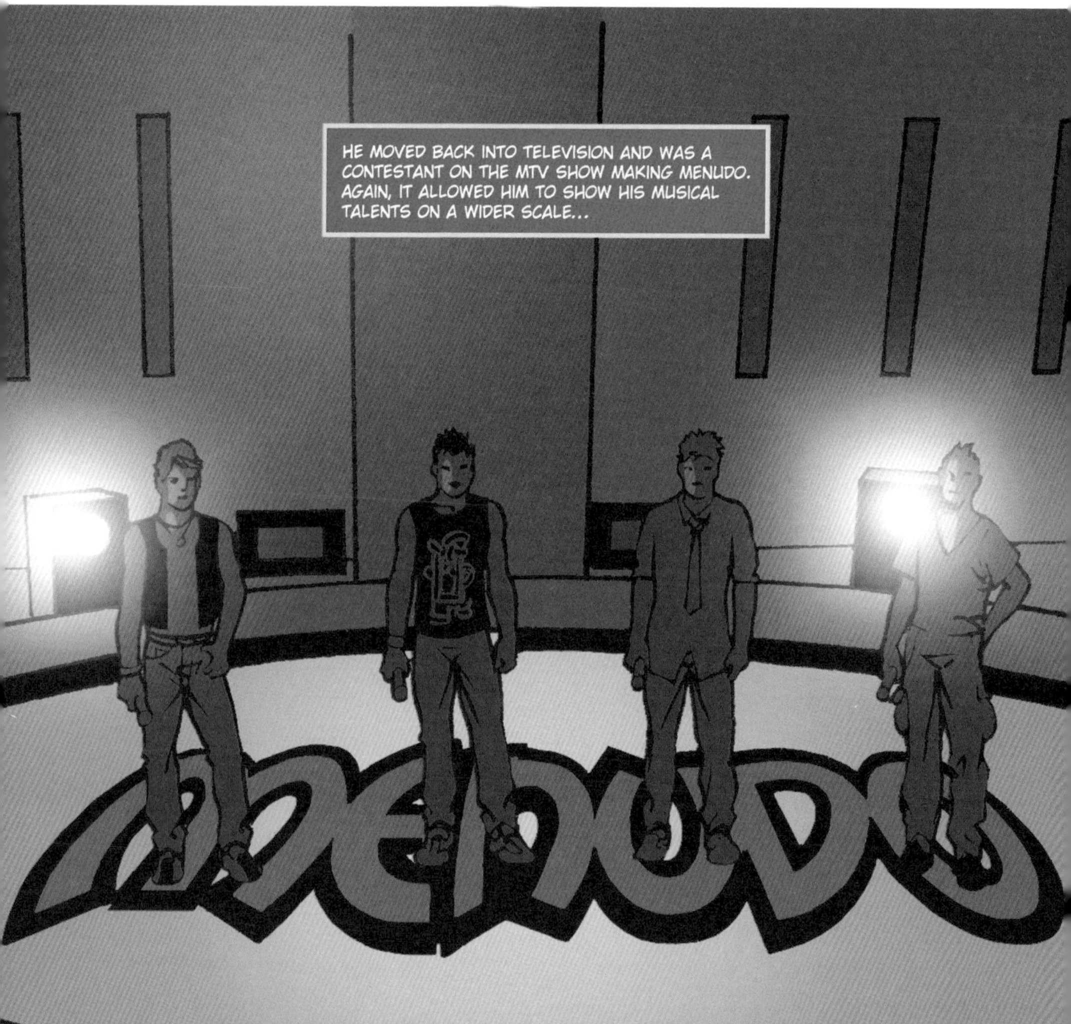
HE MOVED BACK INTO TELEVISION AND WAS A CONTESTANT ON THE MTV SHOW MAKING MENUDO. AGAIN, IT ALLOWED HIM TO SHOW HIS MUSICAL TALENTS ON A WIDER SCALE...
MENUDO

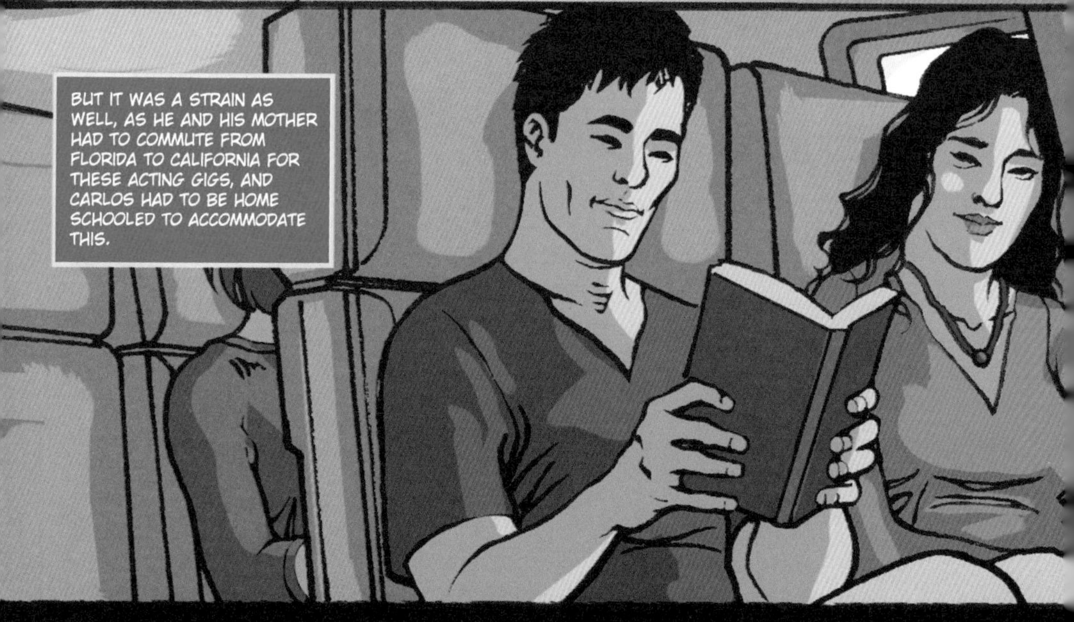
BUT IT WAS A STRAIN AS WELL, AS HE AND HIS MOTHER HAD TO COMMUTE FROM FLORIDA TO CALIFORNIA FOR THESE ACTING GIGS, AND CARLOS HAD TO BE HOME SCHOOLED TO ACCOMMODATE THIS.

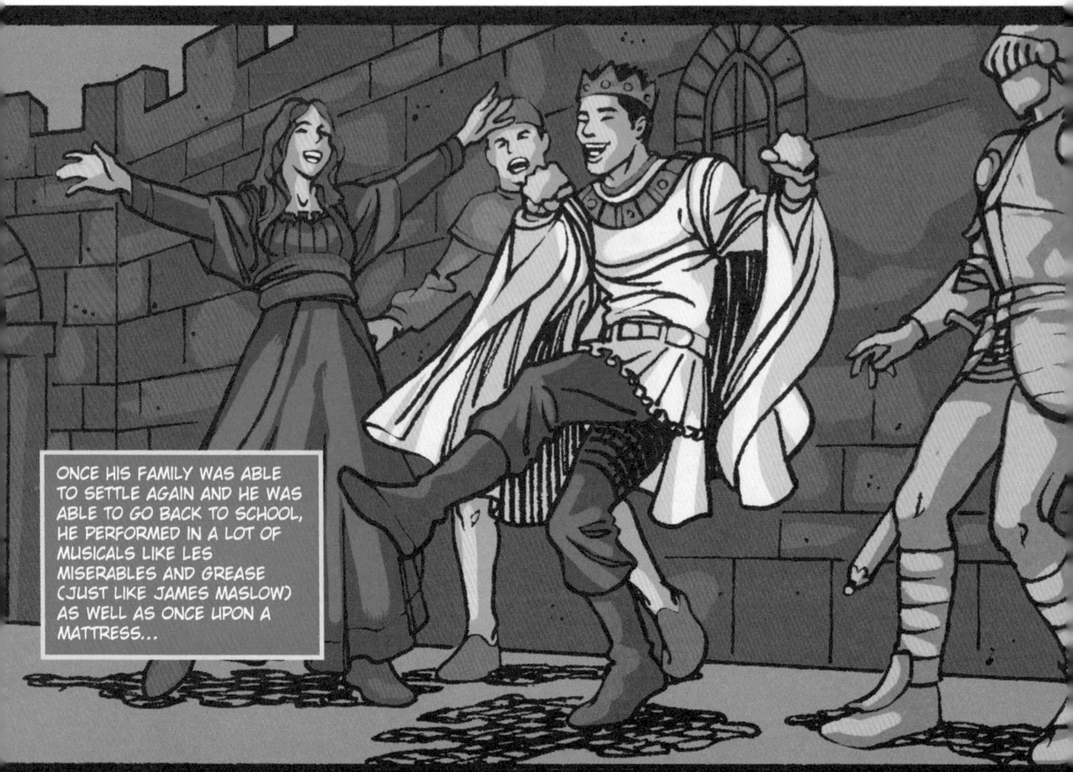
ONCE HIS FAMILY WAS ABLE TO SETTLE AGAIN AND HE WAS ABLE TO GO BACK TO SCHOOL, HE PERFORMED IN A LOT OF MUSICALS LIKE LES MISERABLES AND GREASE (JUST LIKE JAMES MASLOW) AS WELL AS ONCE UPON A MATTRESS...

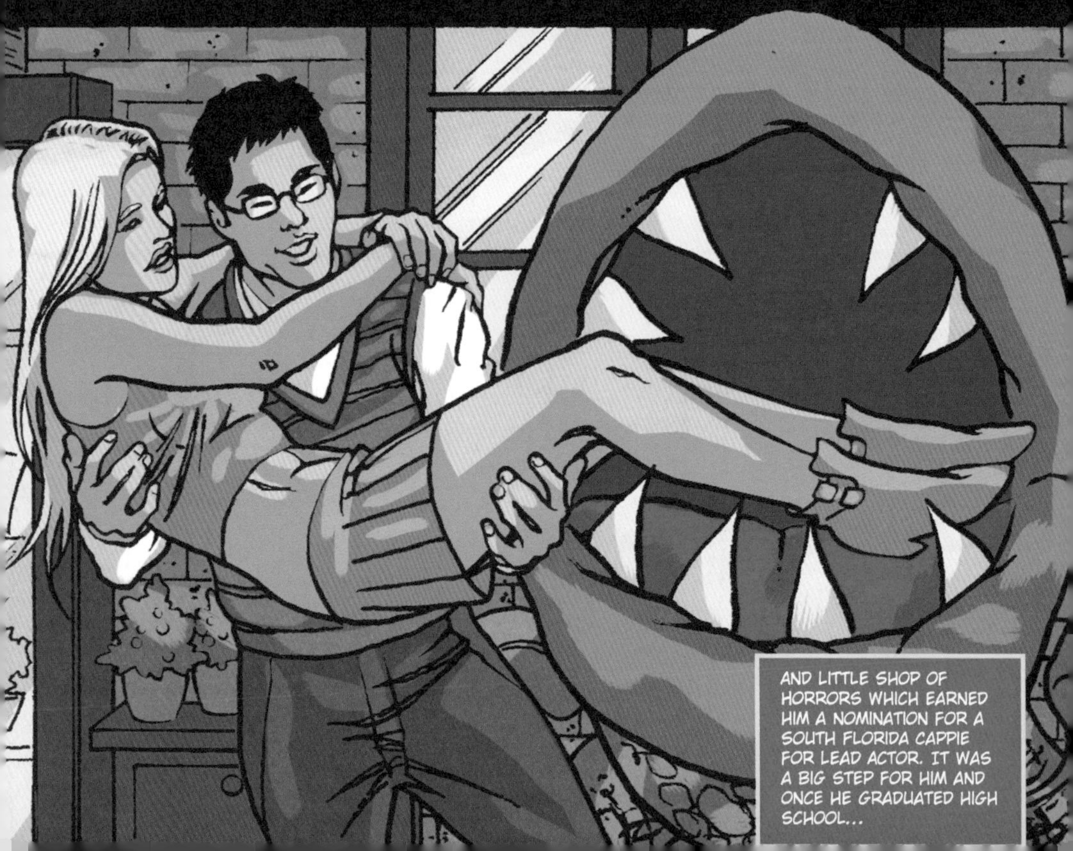
AND LITTLE SHOP OF HORRORS WHICH EARNED HIM A NOMINATION FOR A SOUTH FLORIDA CAPPIE FOR LEAD ACTOR. IT WAS A BIG STEP FOR HIM AND ONCE HE GRADUATED HIGH SCHOOL...

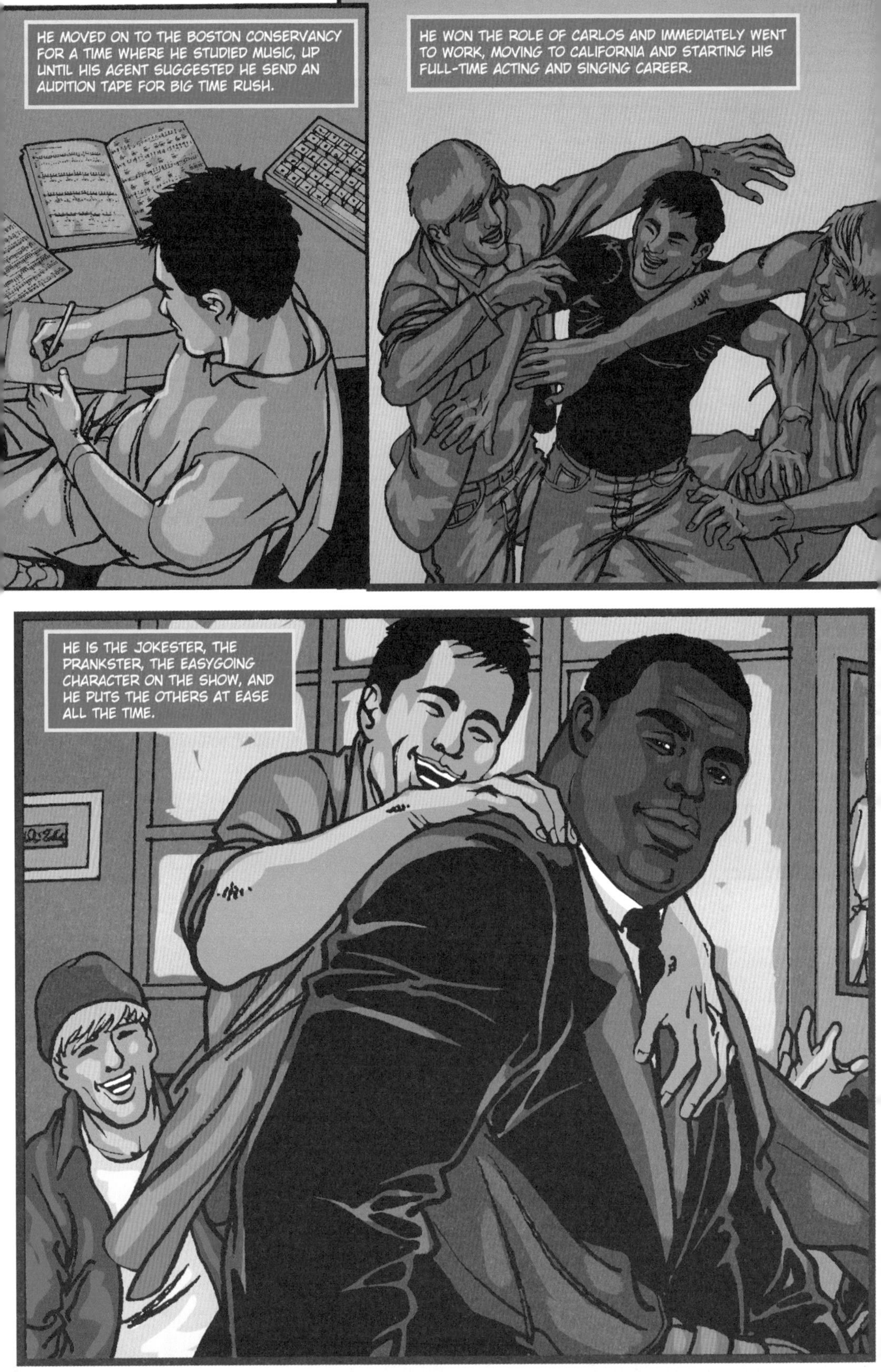
HE MOVED ON TO THE BOSTON CONSERVANCY FOR A TIME WHERE HE STUDIED MUSIC, UP UNTIL HIS AGENT SUGGESTED HE SEND AN AUDITION TAPE FOR BIG TIME RUSH.
HE WON THE ROLE OF CARLOS AND IMMEDIATELY WENT TO WORK, MOVING TO CALIFORNIA AND STARTING HIS FULL-TIME ACTING AND SINGING CAREER.
HE IS THE JOKESTER, THE PRANKSTER, THE EASYGOING CHARACTER ON THE SHOW, AND HE PUTS THE OTHERS AT EASE ALL THE TIME.

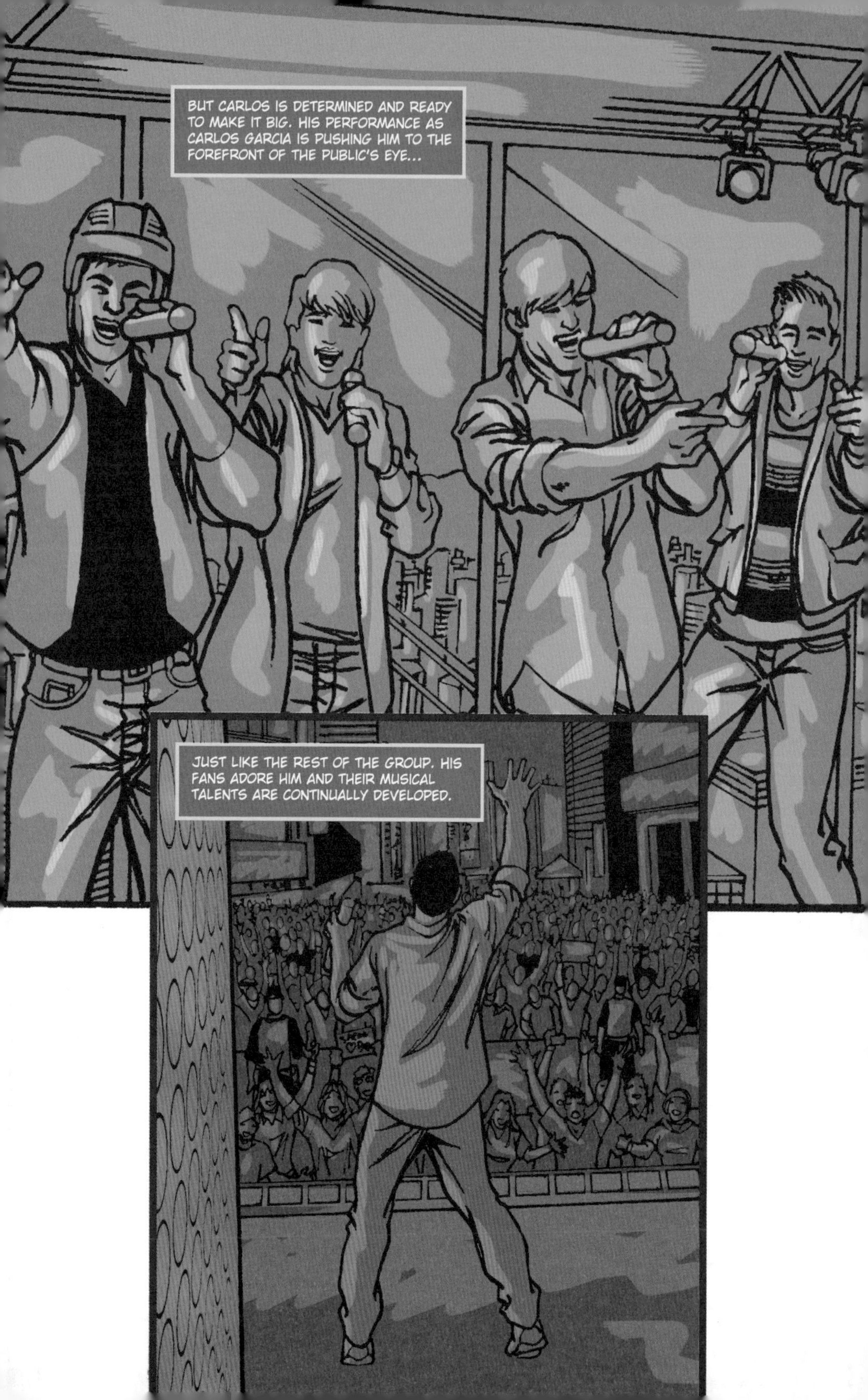
BUT CARLOS IS DETERMINED AND READY TO MAKE IT BIG. HIS PERFORMANCE AS CARLOS GARCIA IS PUSHING HIM TO THE FOREFRONT OF THE PUBLIC'S EYE...
JUST LIKE THE REST OF THE GROUP. HIS FANS ADORE HIM AND THEIR MUSICAL TALENTS ARE CONTINUALLY DEVELOPED.

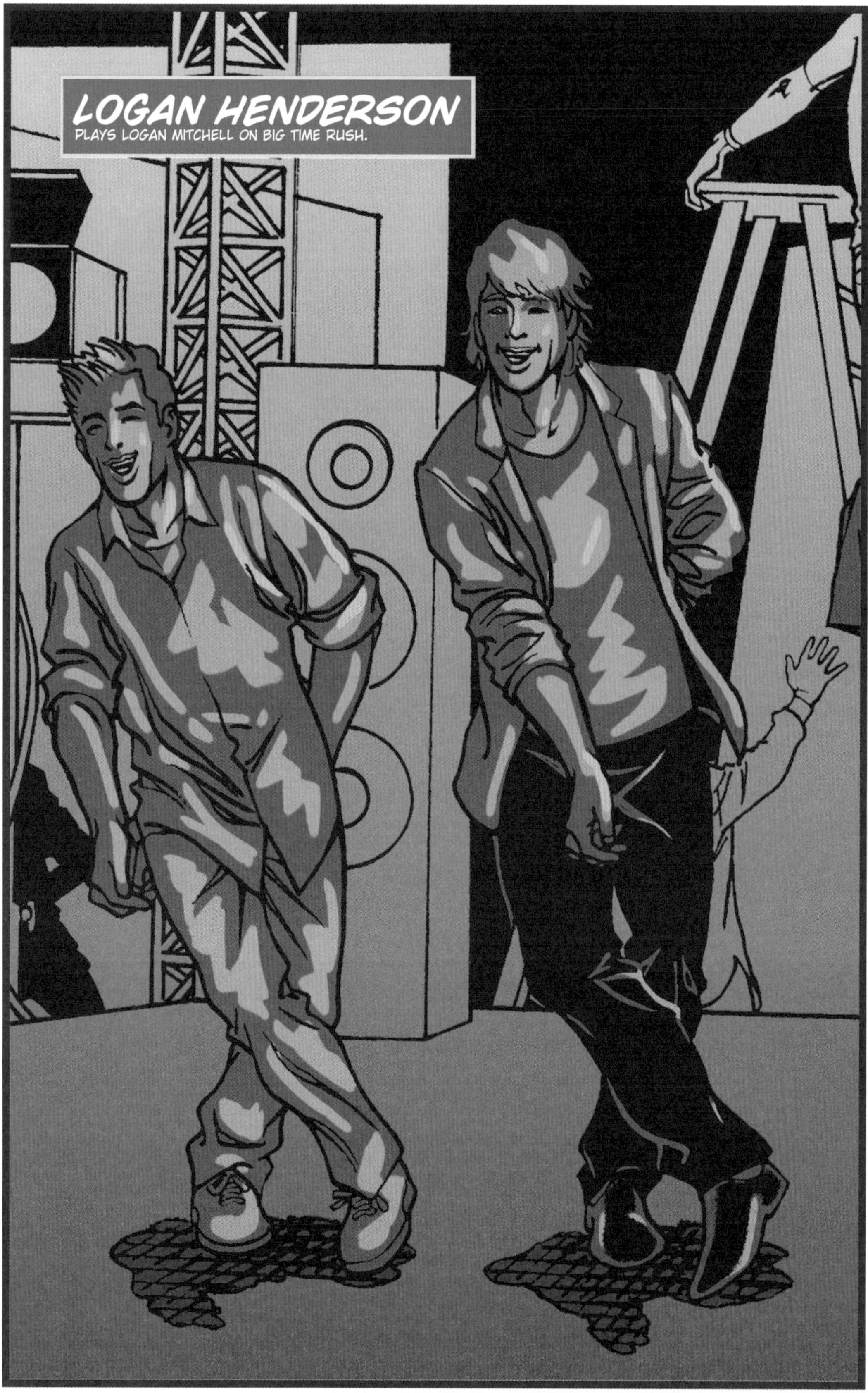
LOGAN HENDERSON
PLAYS LOGAN MITCHELL ON BIG TIME RUSH.

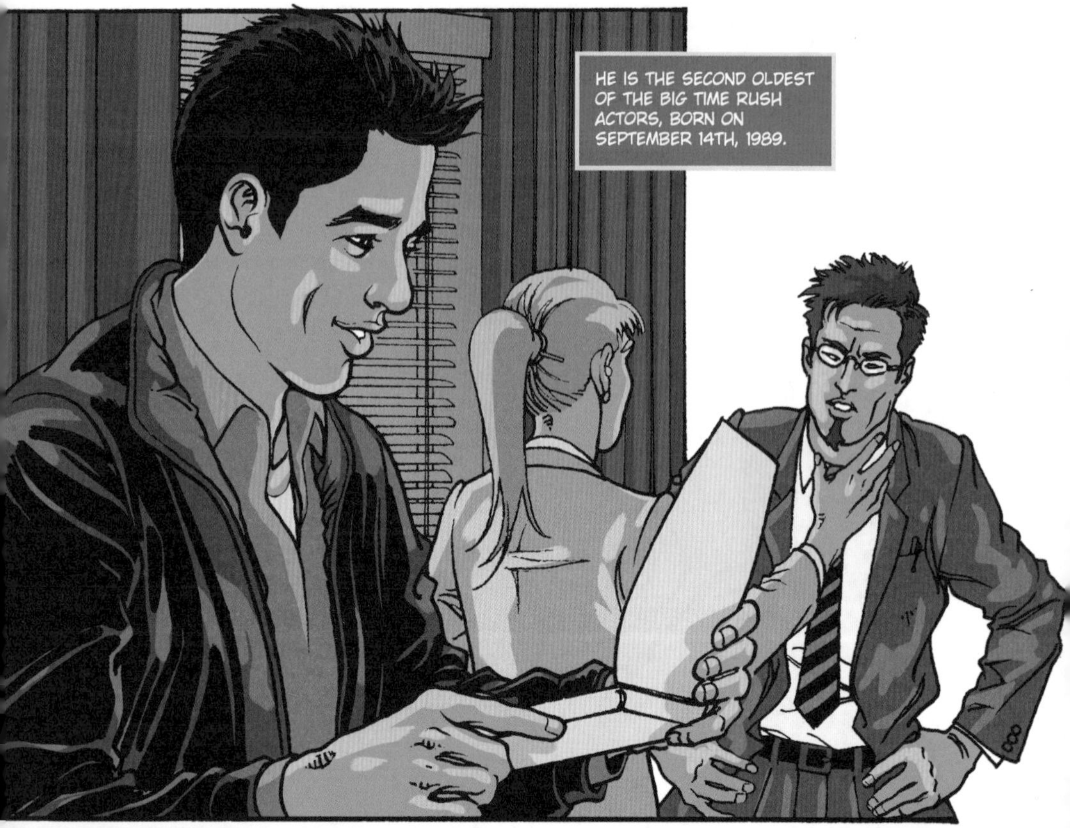
HE IS THE SECOND OLDEST OF THE BIG TIME RUSH ACTORS, BORN ON SEPTEMBER 14TH, 1989.

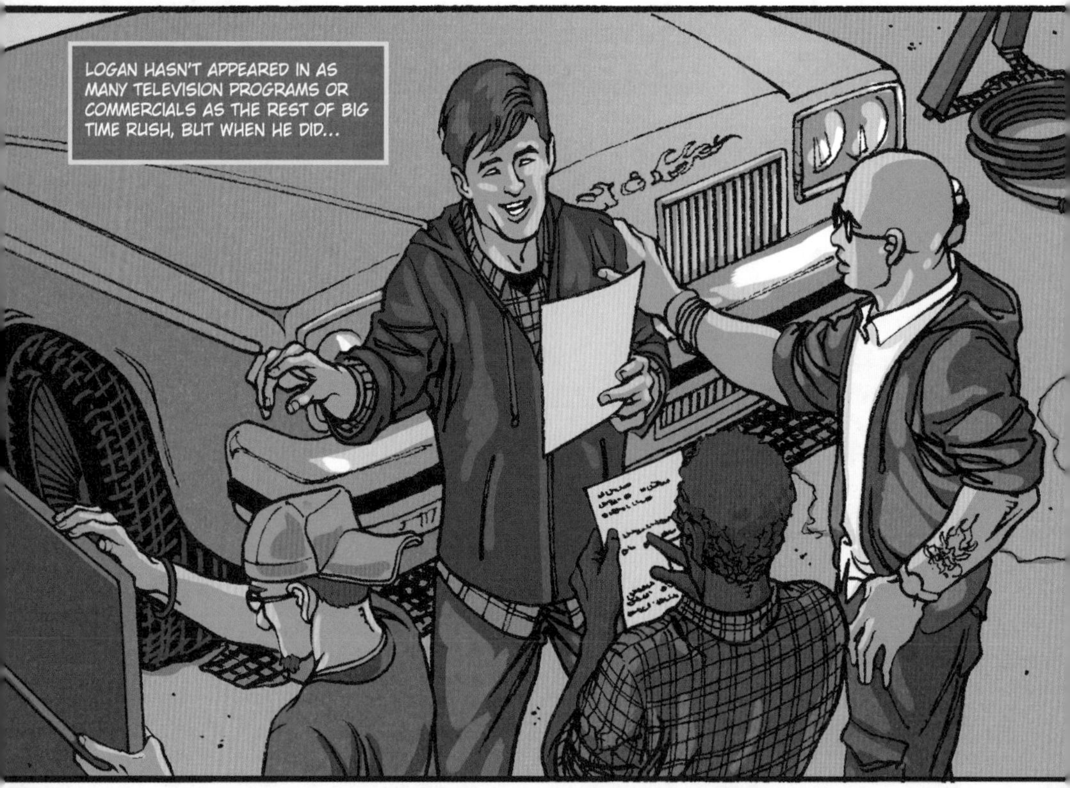
LOGAN HASN'T APPEARED IN AS MANY TELEVISION PROGRAMS OR COMMERCIALS AS THE REST OF BIG TIME RUSH, BUT WHEN HE DID...

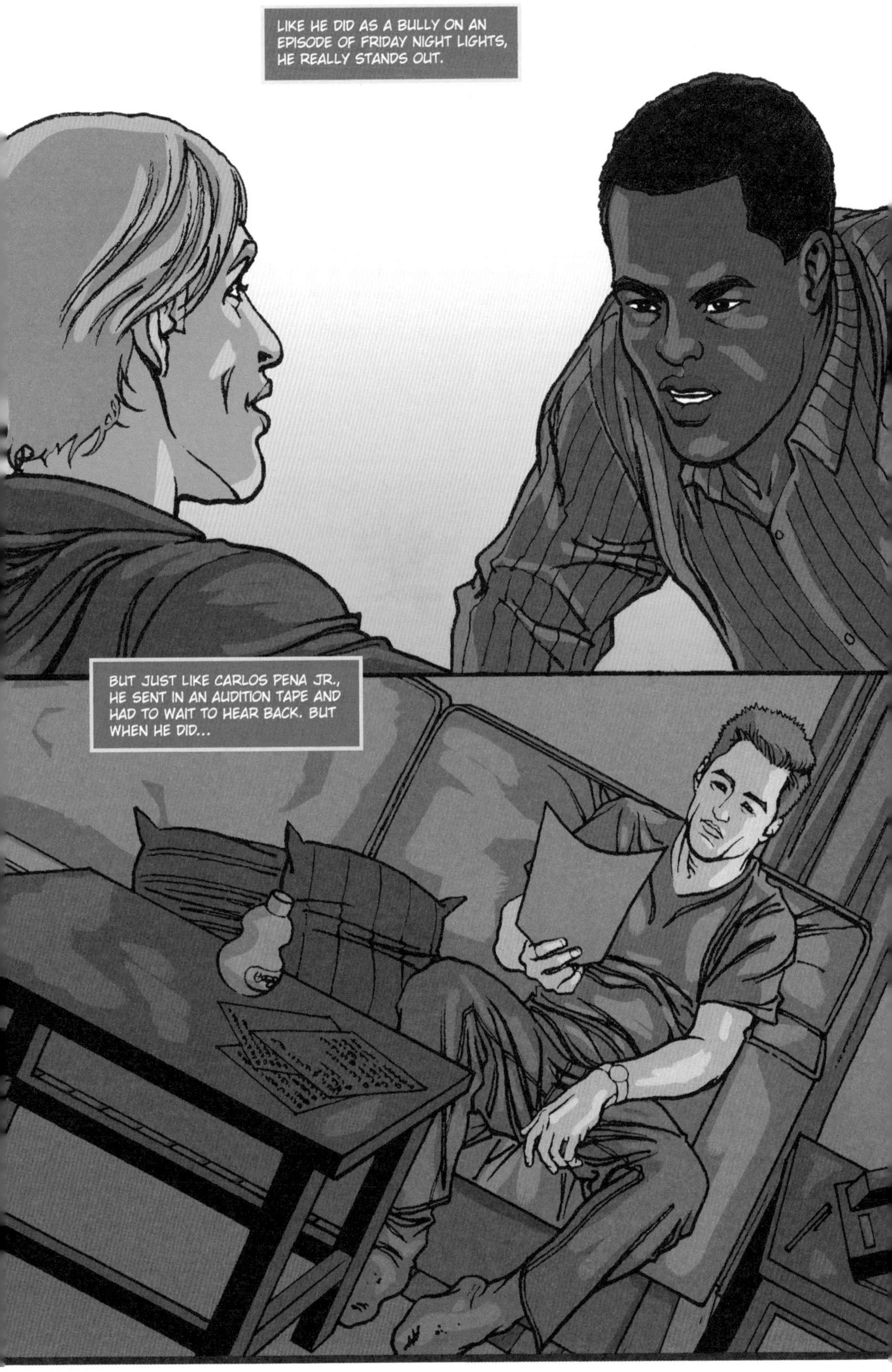
LIKE HE DID AS A BULLY ON AN EPISODE OF FRIDAY NIGHT LIGHTS, HE REALLY STANDS OUT.
BUT JUST LIKE CARLOS PENA JR., HE SENT IN AN AUDITION TAPE AND HAD TO WAIT TO HEAR BACK. BUT WHEN HE DID...

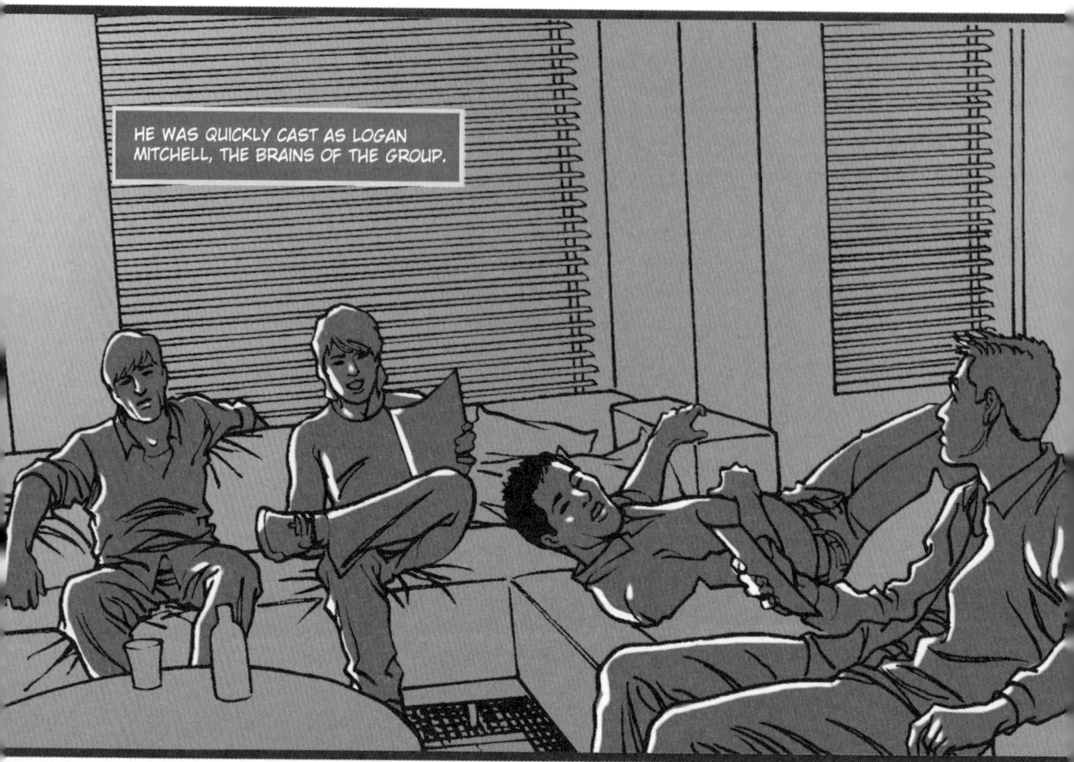
HE WAS QUICKLY CAST AS LOGAN MITCHELL, THE BRAINS OF THE GROUP.

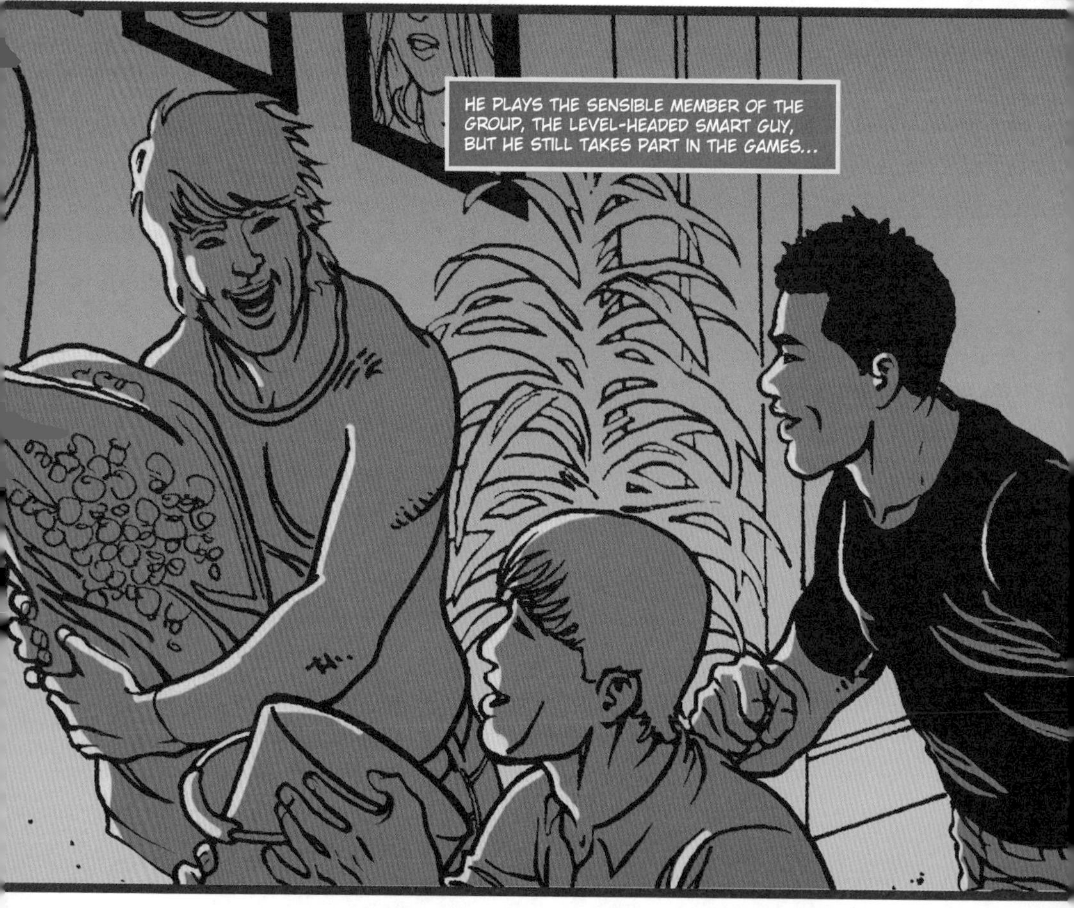
HE PLAYS THE SENSIBLE MEMBER OF THE GROUP, THE LEVEL-HEADED SMART GUY, BUT HE STILL TAKES PART IN THE GAMES...

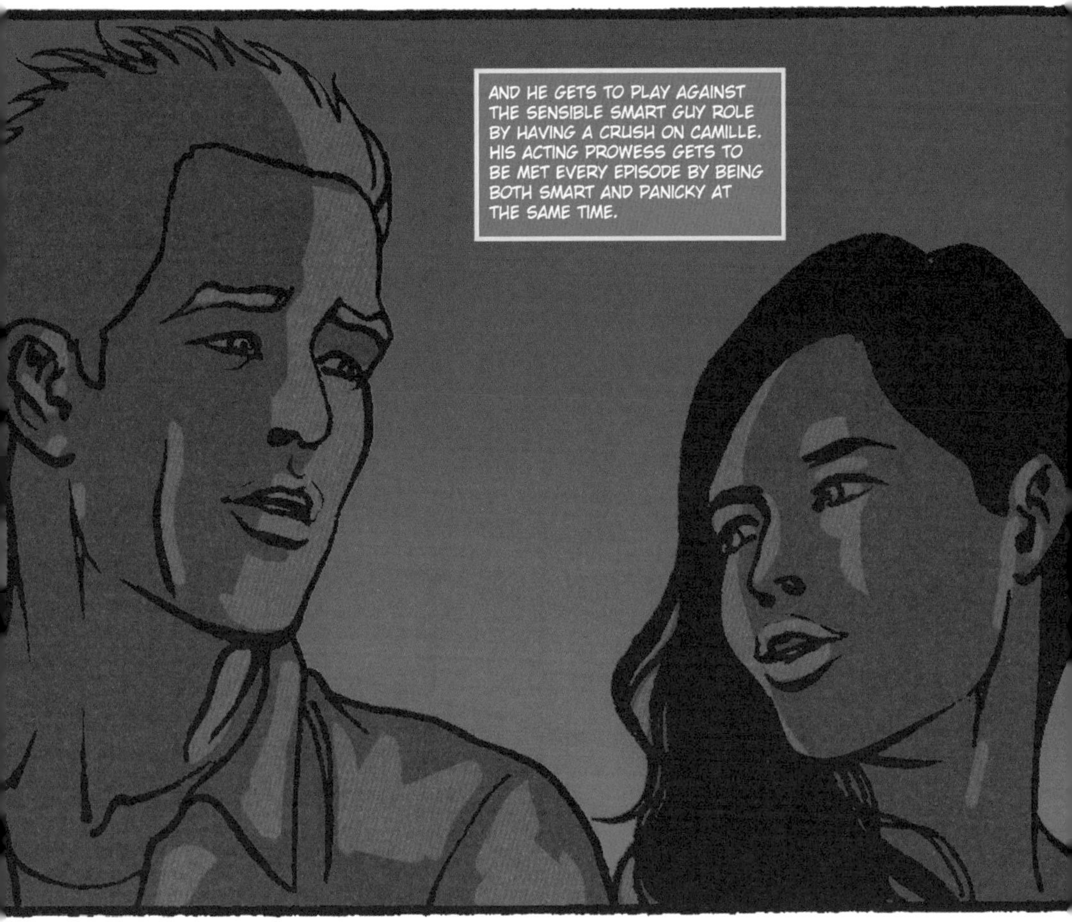
AND HE GETS TO PLAY AGAINST THE SENSIBLE SMART GUY ROLE BY HAVING A CRUSH ON CAMILLE. HIS ACTING PROWESS GETS TO BE MET EVERY EPISODE BY BEING BOTH SMART AND PANICKY AT THE SAME TIME.

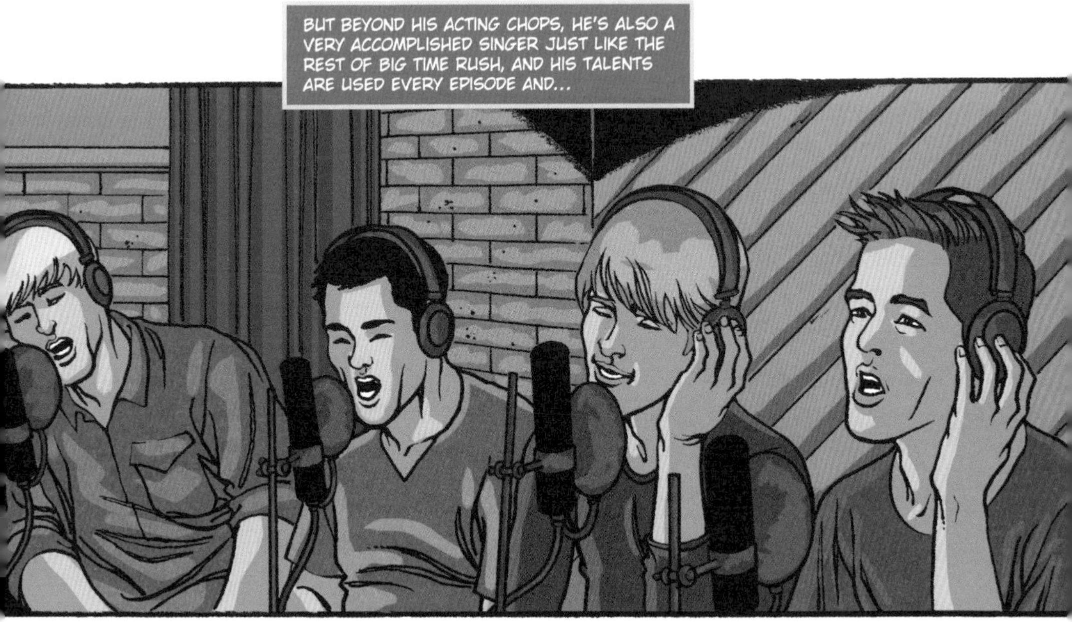
BUT BEYOND HIS ACTING CHOPS, HE'S ALSO A VERY ACCOMPLISHED SINGER JUST LIKE THE REST OF BIG TIME RUSH, AND HIS TALENTS ARE USED EVERY EPISODE AND...

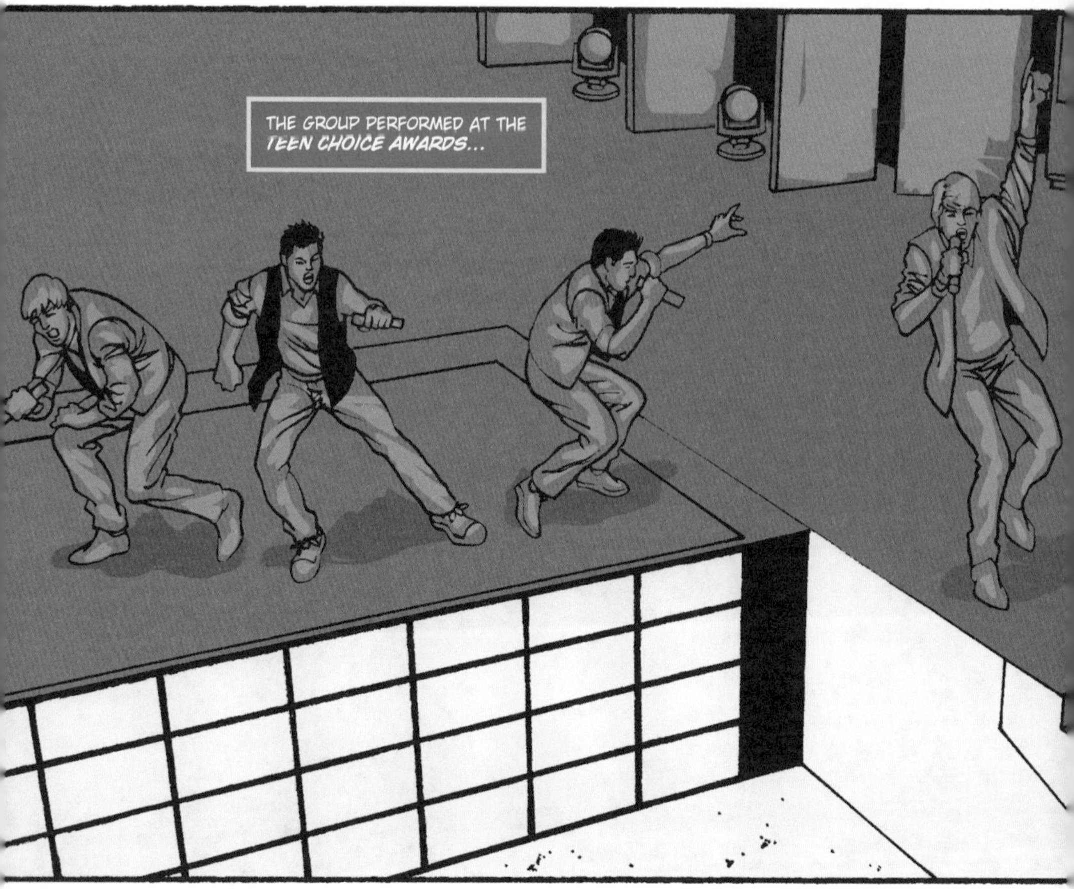
THE GROUP PERFORMED AT THE
TEEN CHOICE AWARDS...

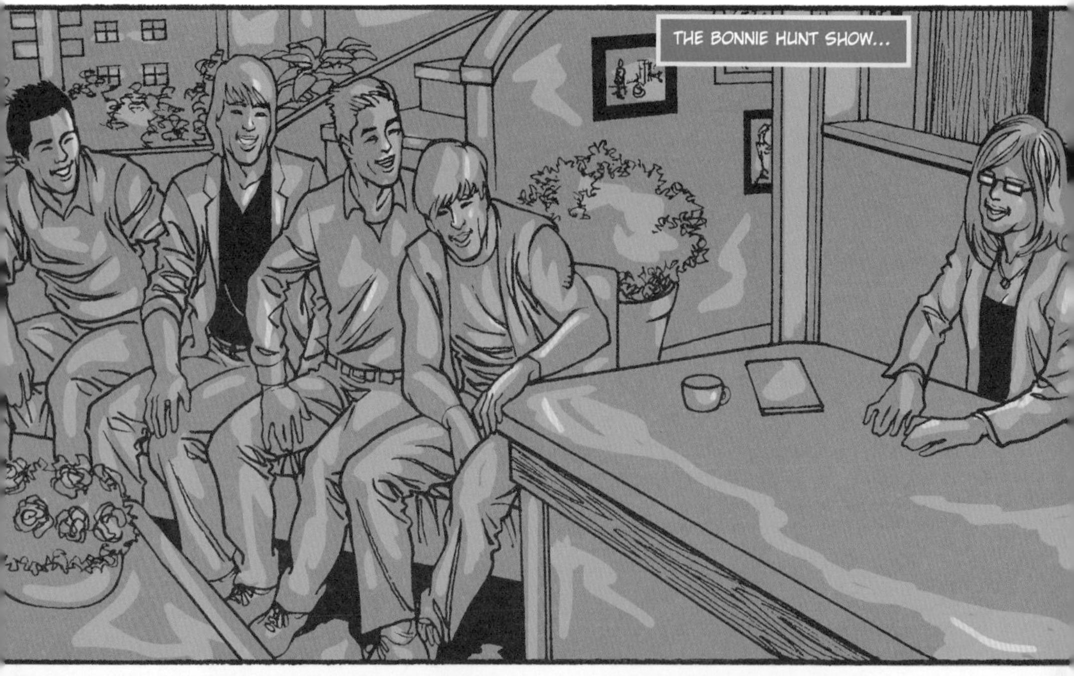
THE BONNIE HUNT SHOW...

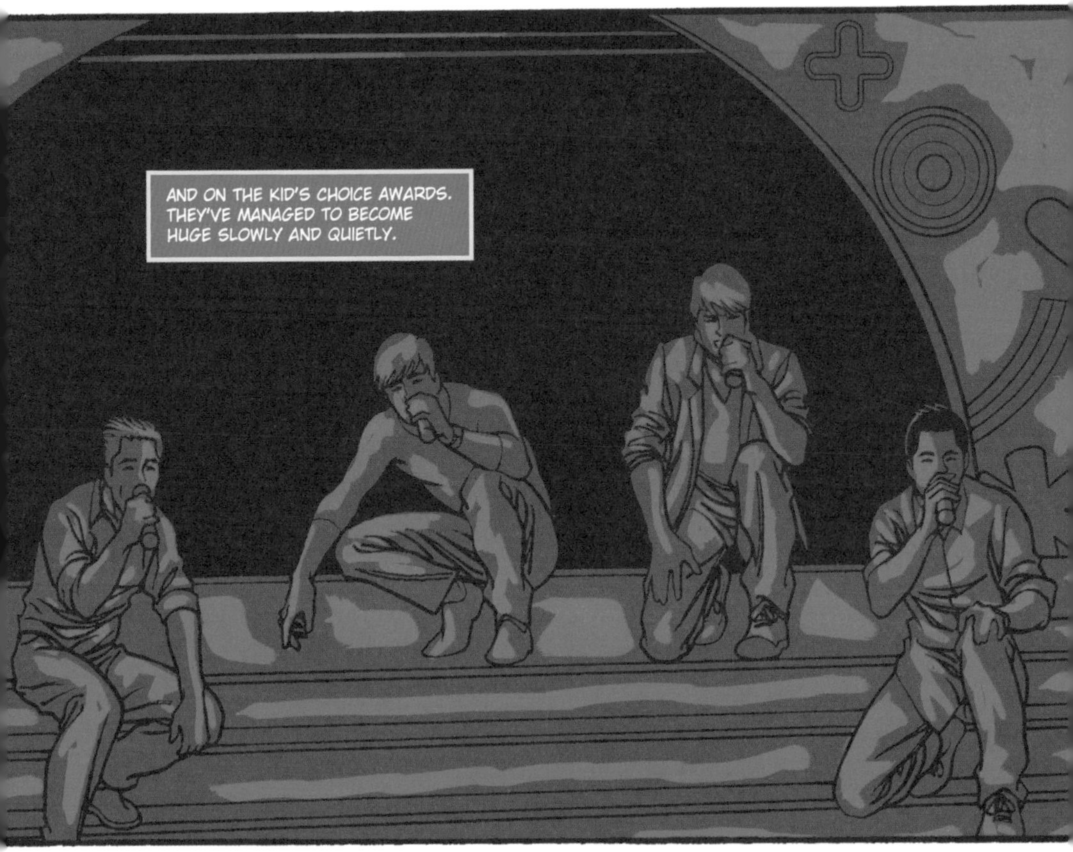
AND ON THE KID'S CHOICE AWARDS. THEY'VE MANAGED TO BECOME HUGE SLOWLY AND QUIETLY.

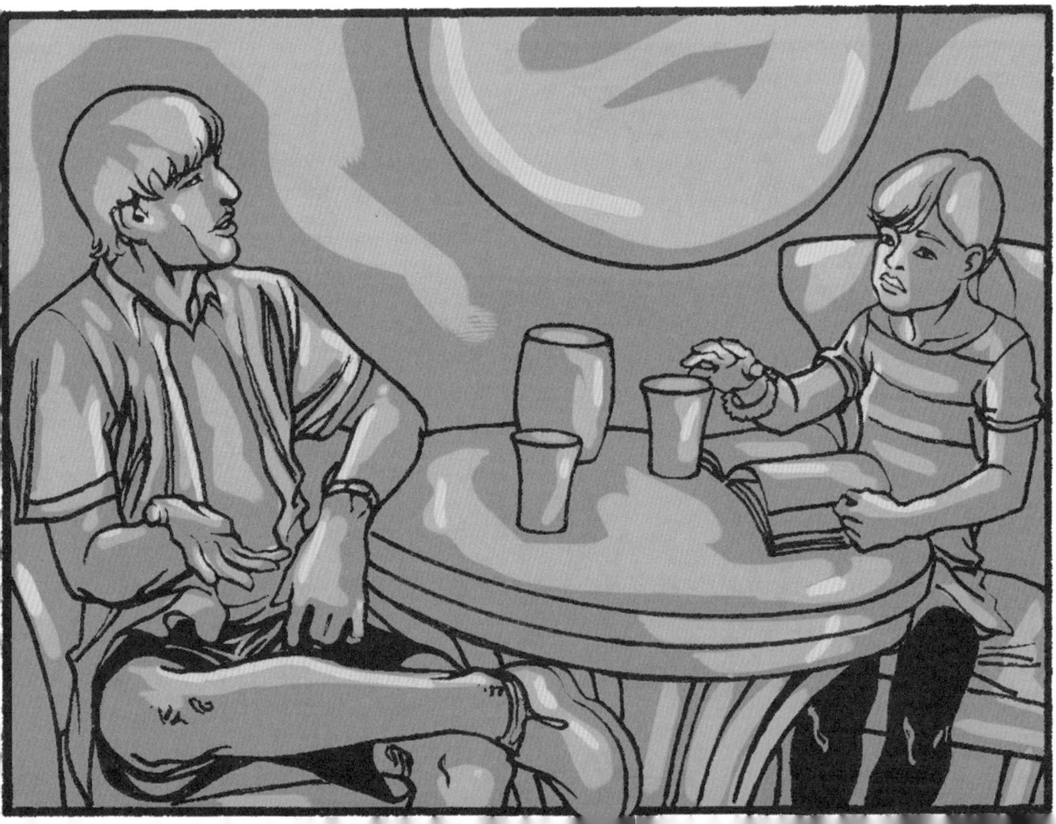

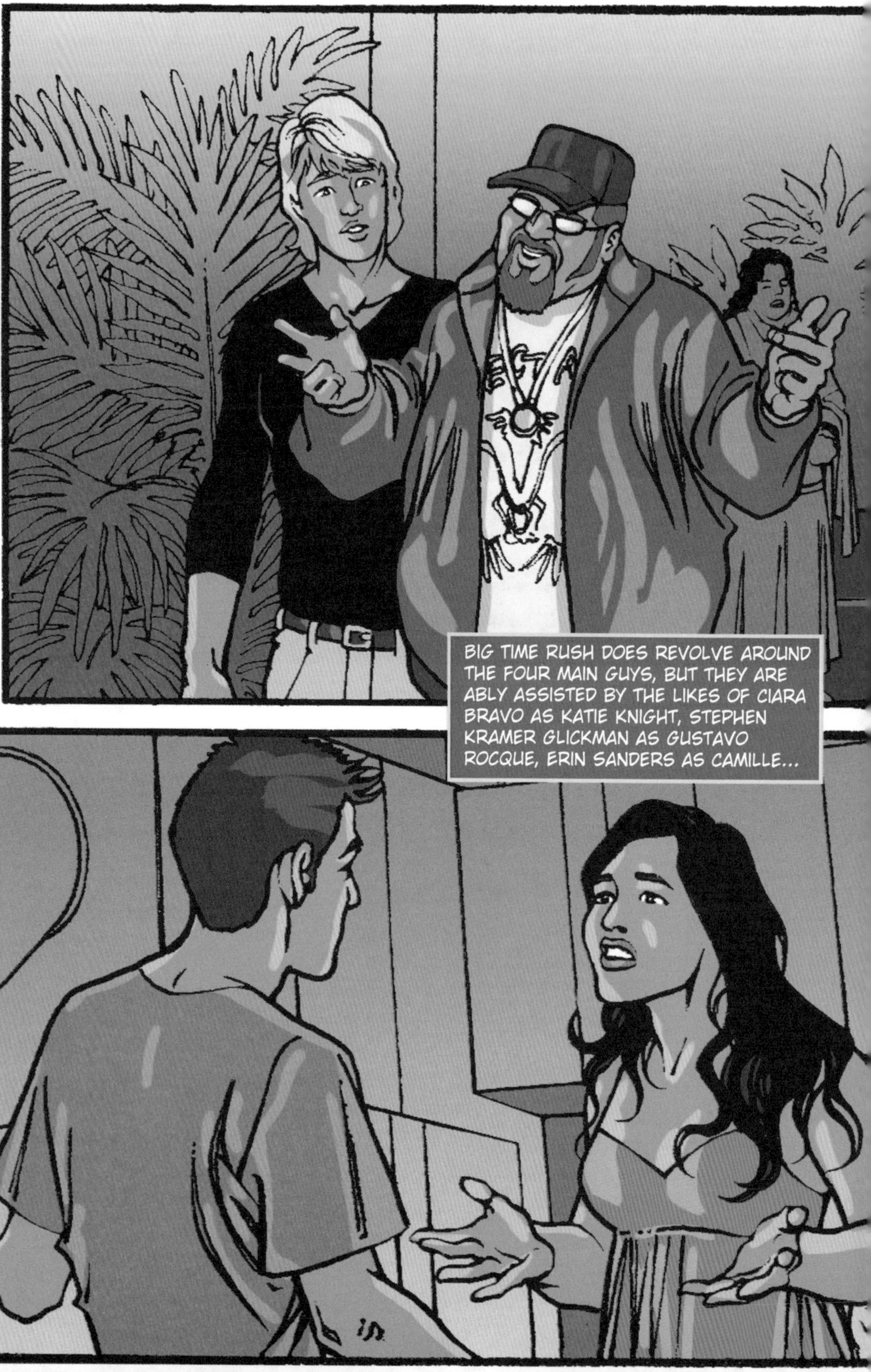
BIG TIME RUSH DOES REVOLVE AROUND THE FOUR MAIN GUYS, BUT THEY ARE ABLY ASSISTED BY THE LIKES OF CIARA BRAVO AS KATIE KNIGHT, STEPHEN KRAMER GLICKMAN AS GUSTAVO ROCQUE, ERIN SANDERS AS CAMILLE...

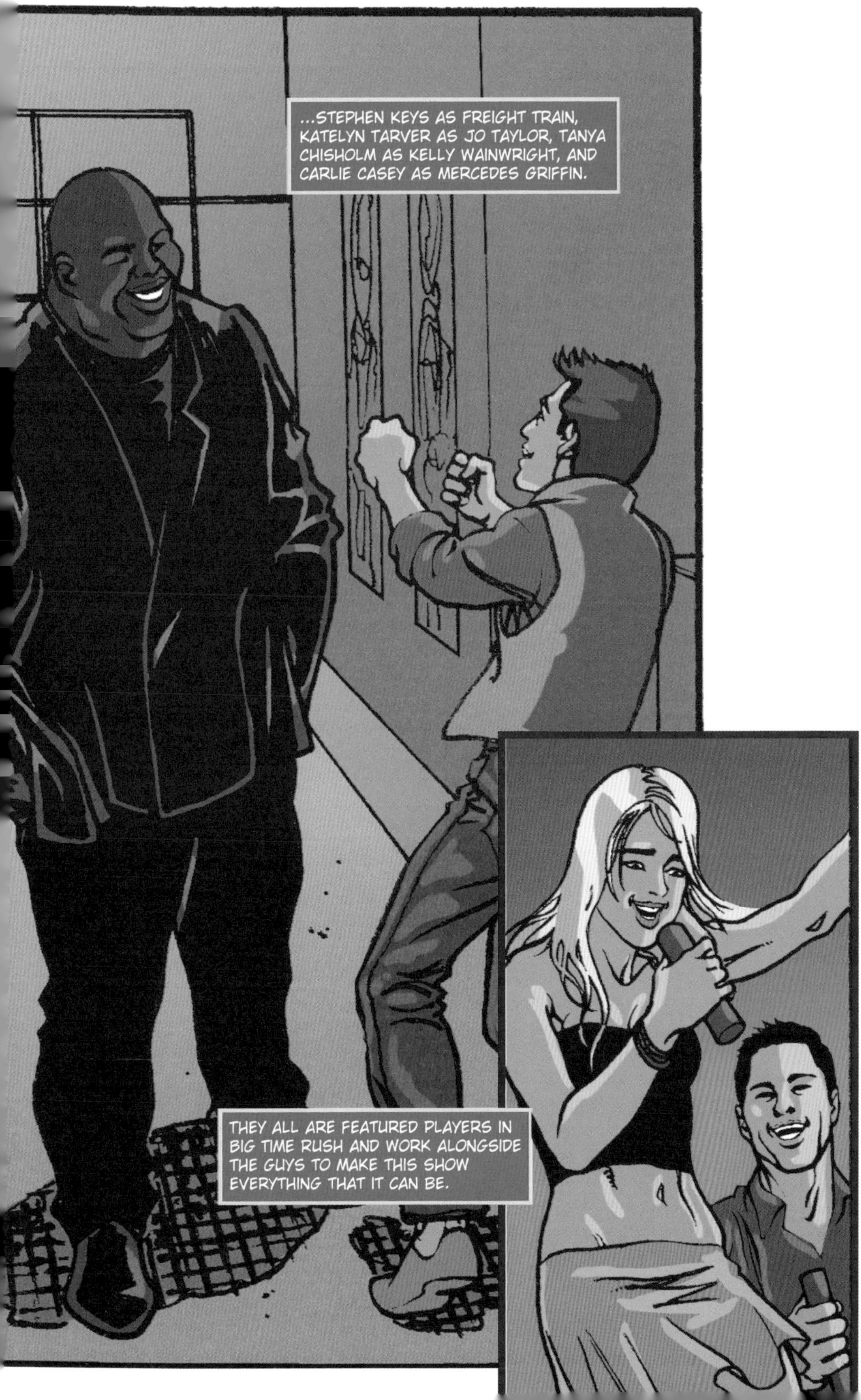
...STEPHEN KEYS AS FREIGHT TRAIN, KATELYN TARVER AS JO TAYLOR, TANYA CHISHOLM AS KELLY WAINWRIGHT, AND CARLIE CASEY AS MERCEDES GRIFFIN.
THEY ALL ARE FEATURED PLAYERS IN BIG TIME RUSH AND WORK ALONGSIDE THE GUYS TO MAKE THIS SHOW EVERYTHING THAT IT CAN BE.

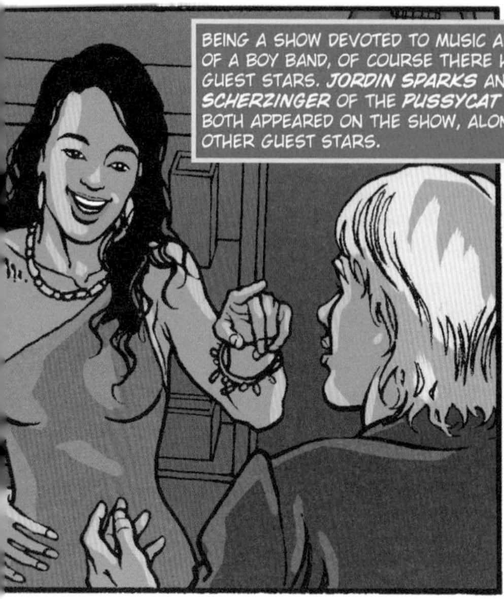
BEING A SHOW DEVOTED TO MUSIC AND THE CREATION OF A BOY BAND, OF COURSE THERE HAVE BEEN GUEST STARS. *JORDIN SPARKS* AND *NICOLE SCHERZINGER* OF THE *PUSSYCAT DOLLS* HAVE BOTH APPEARED ON THE SHOW, ALONGSIDE MANY OTHER GUEST STARS.

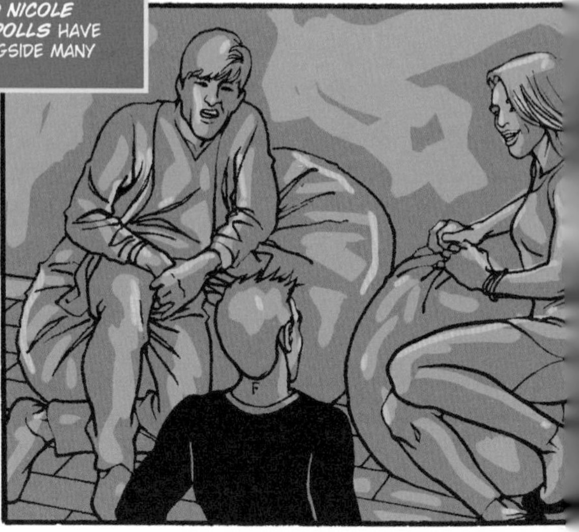

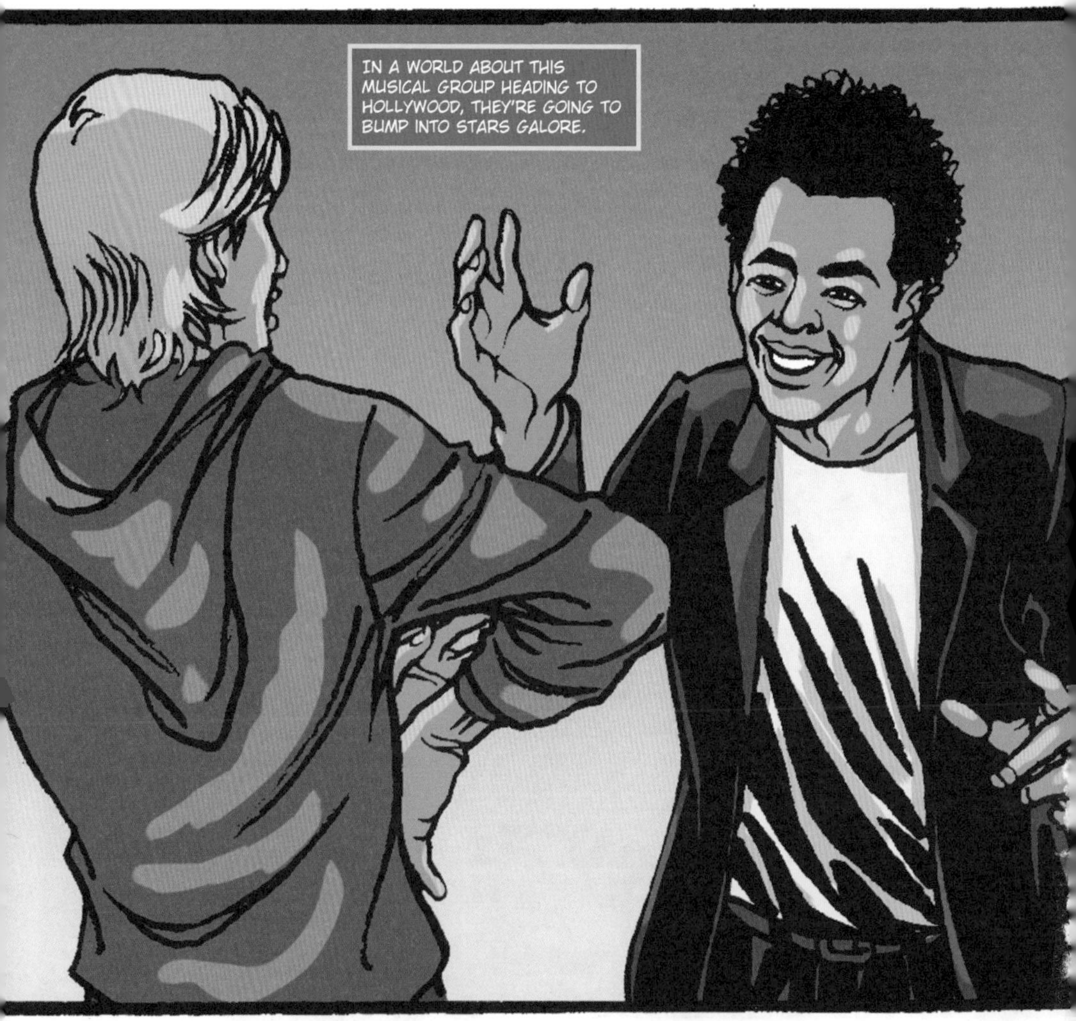
IN A WORLD ABOUT THIS MUSICAL GROUP HEADING TO HOLLYWOOD, THEY'RE GOING TO BUMP INTO STARS GALORE.

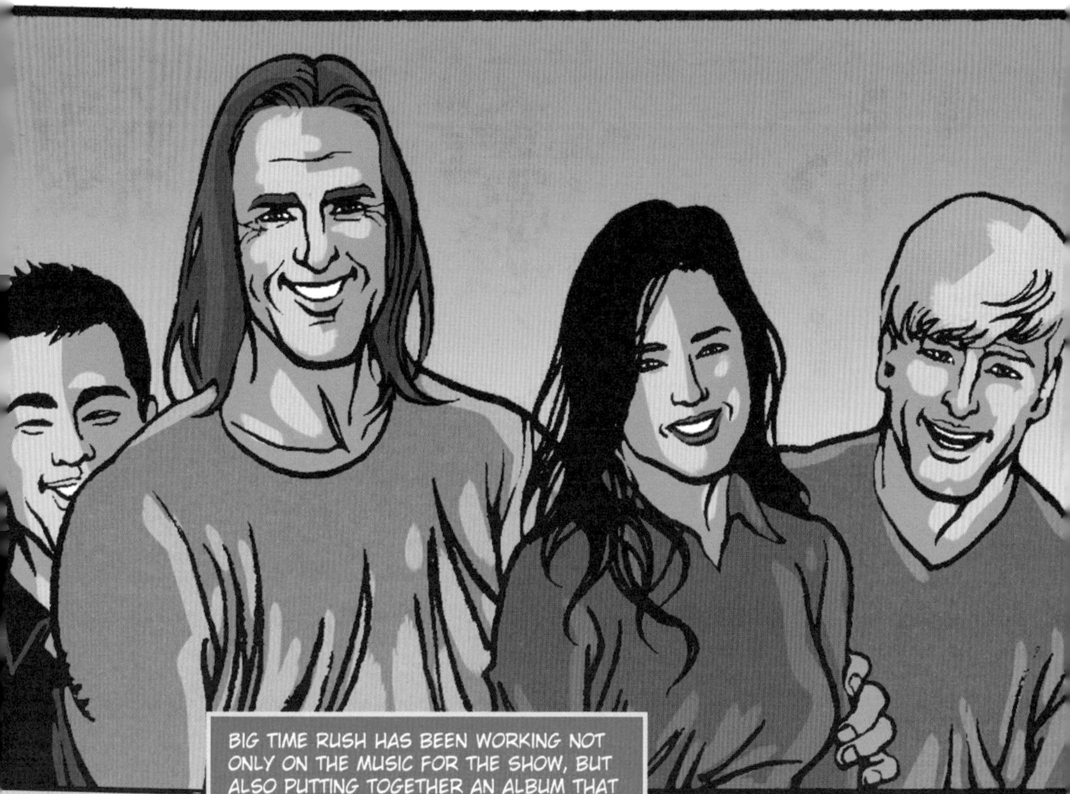

BIG TIME RUSH HAS BEEN WORKING NOT ONLY ON THE MUSIC FOR THE SHOW, BUT ALSO PUTTING TOGETHER AN ALBUM THAT WILL BE RELEASED IN OCTOBER OF 2010.

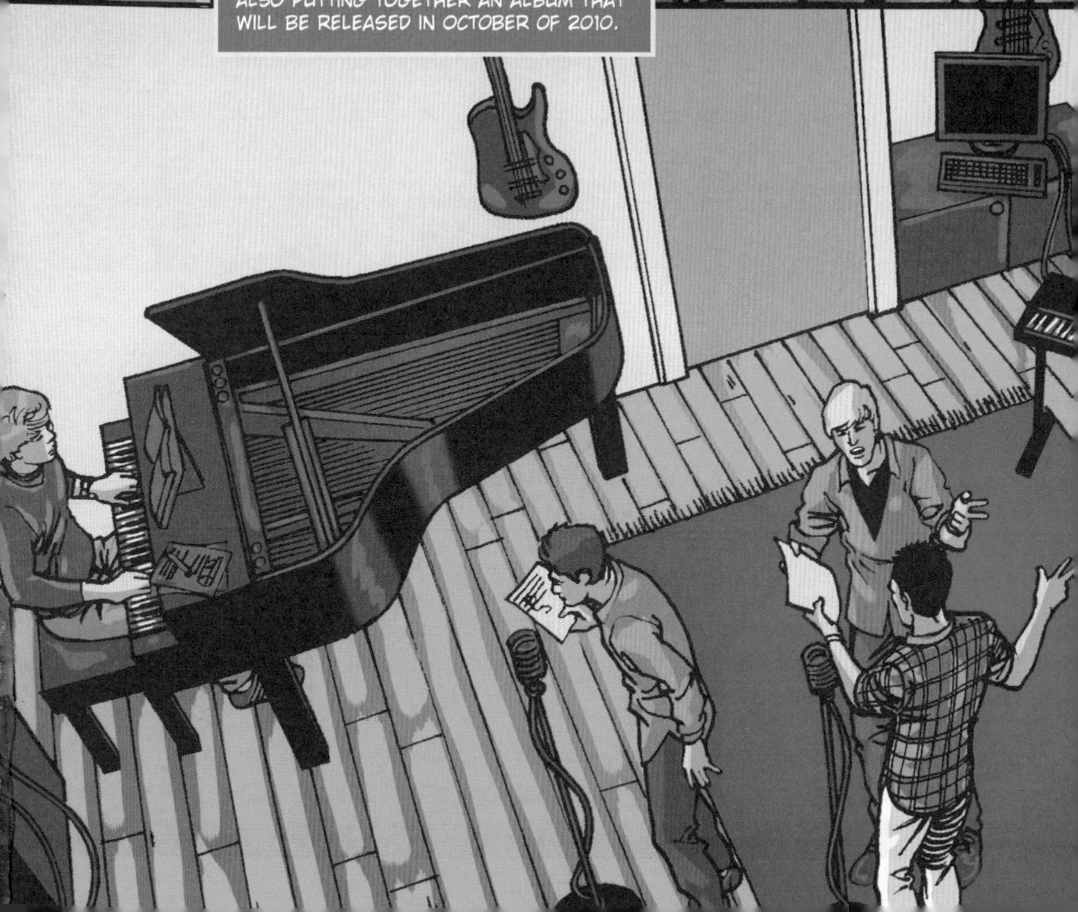

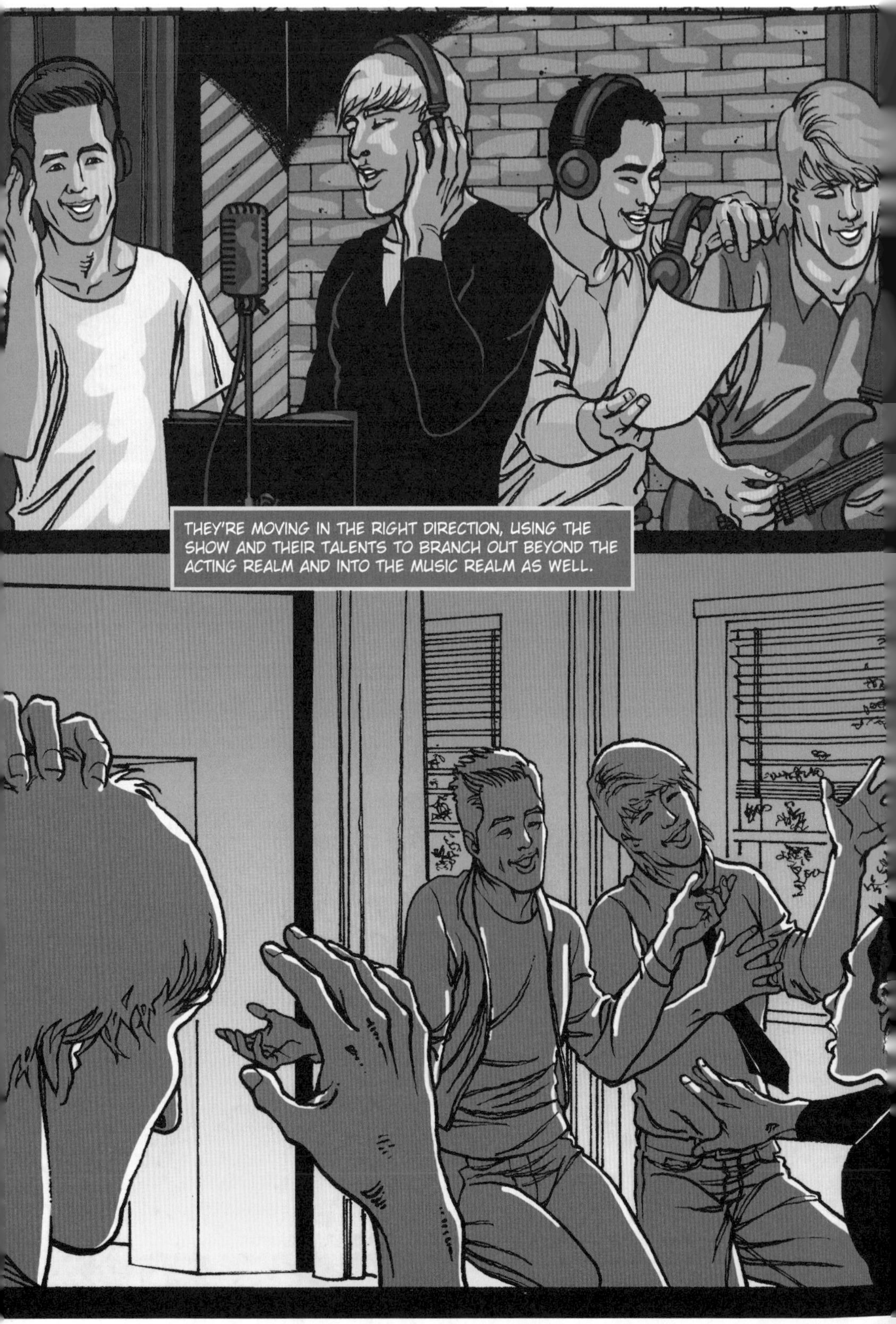
THEY'RE MOVING IN THE RIGHT DIRECTION, USING THE SHOW AND THEIR TALENTS TO BRANCH OUT BEYOND THE ACTING REALM AND INTO THE MUSIC REALM AS WELL.

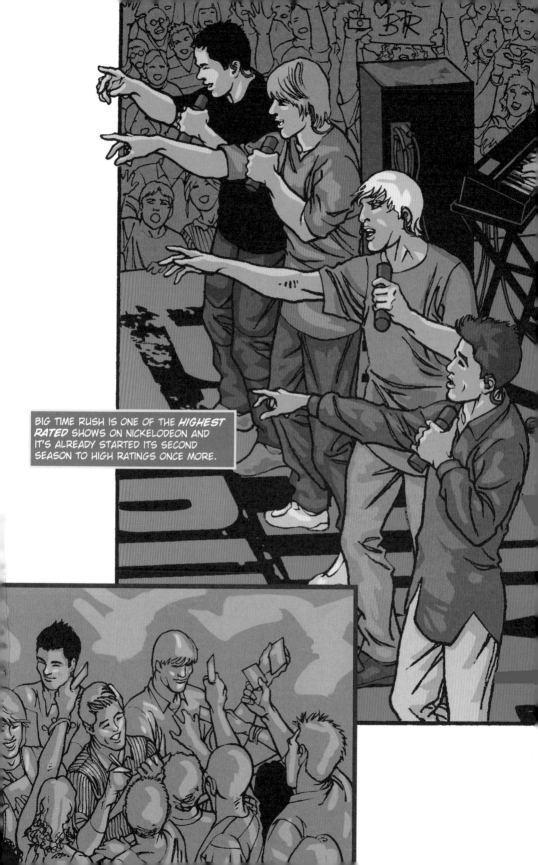

BIG TIME RUSH IS ONE OF THE *HIGHEST RATED* SHOWS ON NICKELODEON AND IT'S ALREADY STARTED ITS SECOND SEASON TO HIGH RATINGS ONCE MORE.

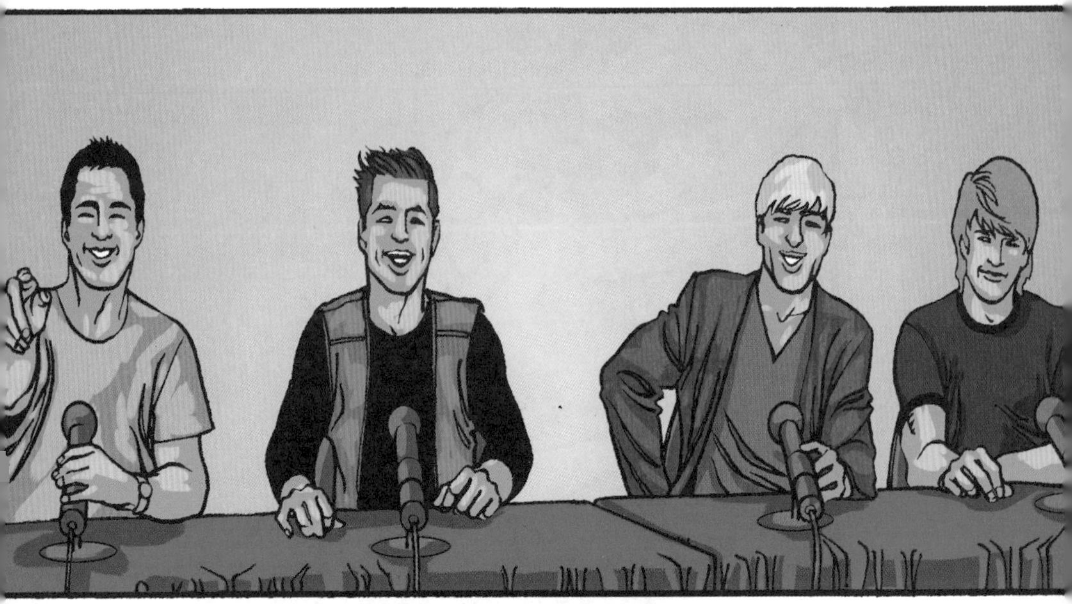

BEYOND THE SHOW ITSELF, THE GROUP IS PLANNING THEIR ***FIRST TOUR***, GOING TO MAJOR VENUES AND MEETING THEIR FANS FACE FIRST. BIG TIME RUSH IS ***REALLY*** HITTING THE BIG TIME...

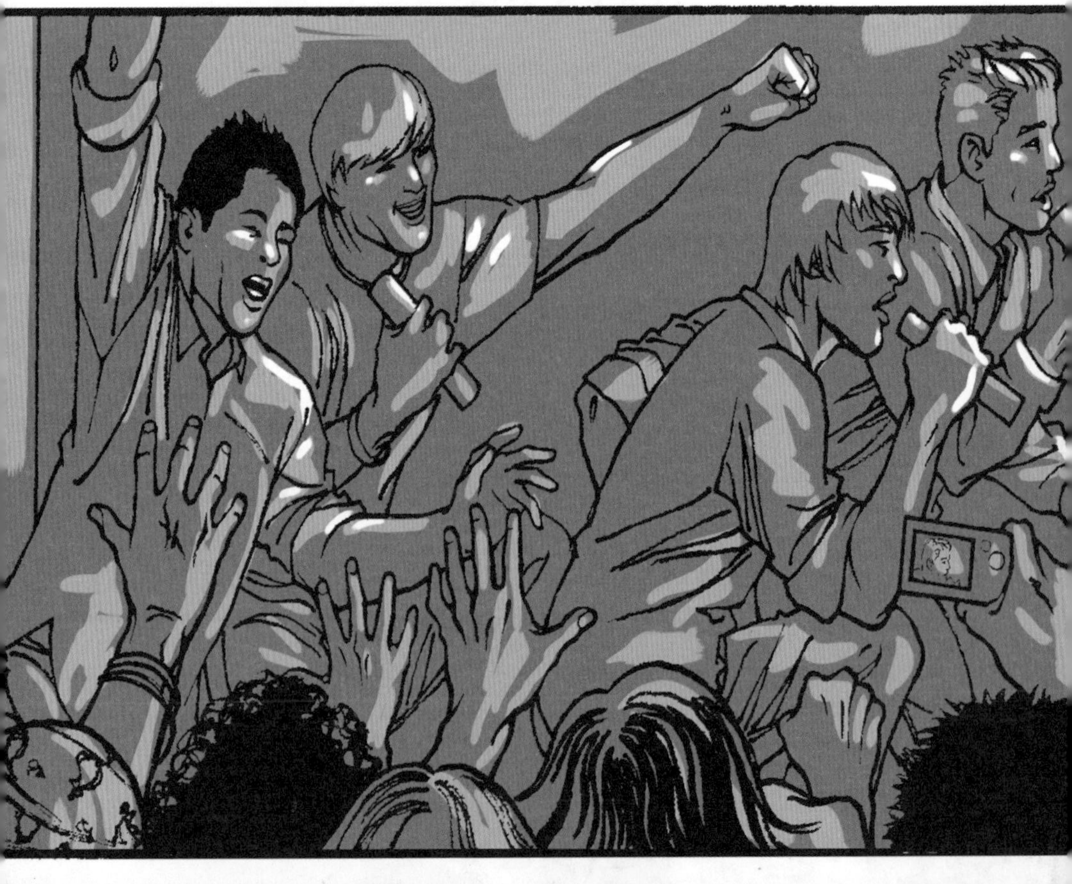

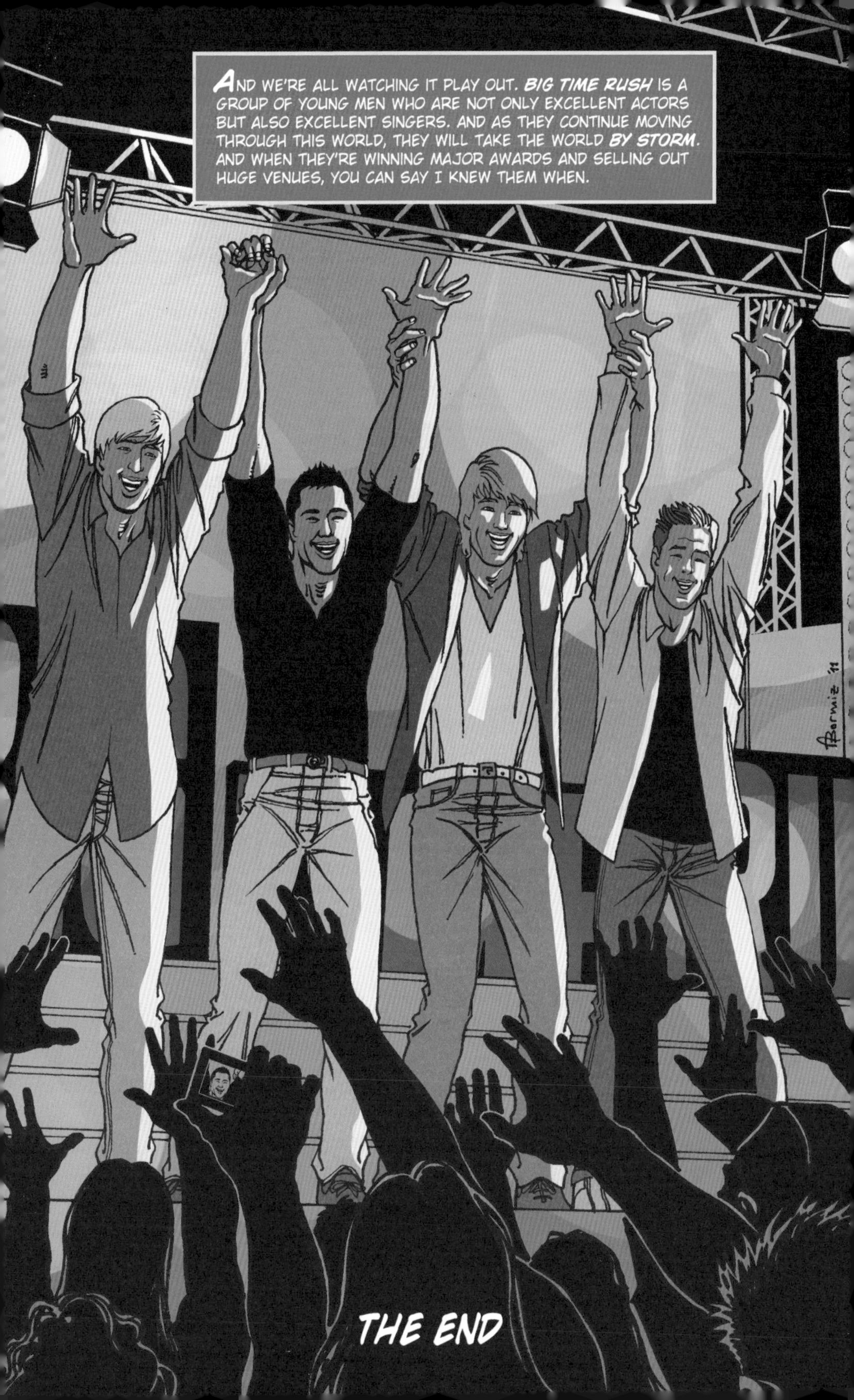
AND WE'RE ALL WATCHING IT PLAY OUT. BIG TIME RUSH IS A GROUP OF YOUNG MEN WHO ARE NOT ONLY EXCELLENT ACTORS BUT ALSO EXCELLENT SINGERS. AND AS THEY CONTINUE MOVING THROUGH THIS WORLD, THEY WILL TAKE THE WORLD BY STORM. AND WHEN THEY'RE WINNING MAJOR AWARDS AND SELLING OUT HUGE VENUES, YOU CAN SAY I KNEW THEM WHEN.
THE END

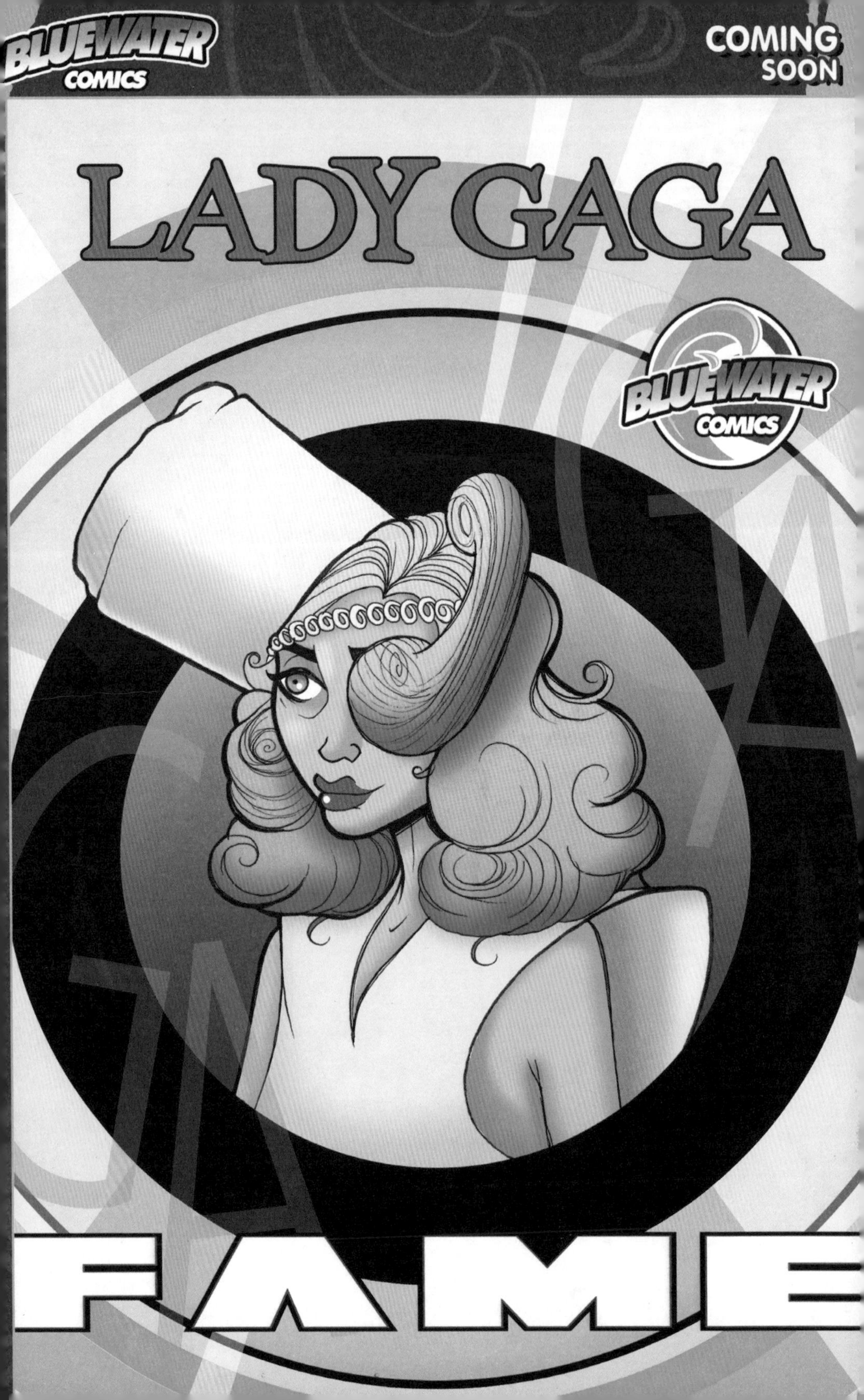
BLUEWATER COMICS
COMING SOON
LADY GAGA
BLUEWATER COMICS
FAME